ZUPPE RISOTTI POLENTA!
Italian Soup, Rice & Polenta Dishes

Mariapaola Dettore
Photography by Marco Lanza
Set Design by Sara Vignozzi

McRAE BOOKS

Other titles in the series
Antipasti! Appetizers the Italian Way
Pastissima! Pasta the Italian Way
Pizza Pane Focacce! Pizza, Bread & Focaccia the Italian Way
Pesce! Seafood the Italian Way
Carne! Meat Dishes the Italian Way
Verdure! Vegetables the Italian Way
Dolci e Frutta! Desserts the Italian Way

ISBN 88-89272-44-9

This book was conceived, edited and designed by McRae Books Srl
Borgo Santa Croce, 8
50122 Florence, Italy
info@mcraebooks.com

Publishers: Marco Nardi & Anne McRae
Text: Mariapaola Dèttore
Photography: Marco Lanza
Set Design: Sara Vignozzi
Design: Marco Nardi
Translation from the Italian: Erika Paoli
Editing: Lynn McRae and Anne McRae
Illustrations: Paola Holguín
Colour separations: Fotolito Toscana, Florence, Italy
Printed and bound in the Slovak Republic by Polygraf Print

The Publishers would like to thank Eugenio Taccini (Montelupo Fiorentino), Flavia Srl (Montelupo Fiorentino), La Tuscia (Lastra a Signa), Enza Bettelli, Alessandro Frassinelli and Leonardo Pasquinelli for their assistance during the production of this book.

CONTENTS

INTRODUCTION

A wide range of first courses are served throughout Italy alongside or in place of pasta. Many share a long and honourable position in Italian culinary tradition. This book offers a broad panorama of these dishes from the various regions. From the lightest of broths, characterised by just a few ingredients, to peasant-style, vegetable-based soups, sometimes with the addition of bread, pasta or rice. Simplicity often means elegance, and there are some wonderful surprises in this chapter. Rice provides a broad sweep of possible combinations. The central and northern regions all have their own secrets for preparing and serving rice and risotti. The infinite variety of tastes and alliances in the recipes here will delight even the most experienced of palates. And to finish, the warmth of golden polenta, a typical winter dish. Polenta too can be served in many and varied ways and is open to a host of fascinating interpretations. Good luck and
Buon Appetito!

CHEESES

Cheese plays a conspicuous role in Italian cuisine and there is an enormous variety of types and brands available throughout the peninsula. These are a selection of the cheeses included in the recipes in this book. Don't be alarmed if you can't find the exact cheese in your local supermarket or speciality shop, use a similar local product in its place.

Pecorino romano

PECORINO
Pecorino comes from central and south Italy. The many different types are all made of sheep's milk. A table cheese until about 8 months of aging, after which it is used to flavour cooked dishes. *Pecorino romano* is the tastiest, while the Tuscan varieties are fuller and sweeter.

Pecorino toscano

TOMA PIEMONTESE
From Piedmont and Val d'Aosta in the north, Toma is made of unfermented cow's milk. Taste varies from very mild to strong, depending on aging which ranges from 1 to 6 months.

PARMIGIANO
The king of Italian cheeses and the most well-known. Perfect for both cooking and as a table cheese. Made of cow's milk, it is aged for 18 months to 4 years.

TALEGGIO
Together with Gorgonzola, it has ancient origins; there are records of its production in Lombardy dating from 1,000 years ago. It is a soft, buttery cheese with a distinctive aromatic flavour.

GORGONZOLA
A creamy northern cheese, it is sharp, tasty and sweet all at once. Made of cow's milk, it is characterised by the blue green veins of tasty mould.

GRUYÈRE
A Swiss cheese which is also produced in the alpine areas of northern Italy. It has an intense and aromatic flavour.

EMMENTAL
One of the best known Swiss cheeses, wide use is made of it in Italian cooking. It has a full, delicate taste and also makes an excellent table cheese.

PROVOLONE
Originally a southern cheese, from Campania, the area around Naples. It is now produced in many regions, each one giving it a special shape. Aging determines taste; the younger varieties are milder and the older ones tasty.

Provolone

MOZZARELLA
From Campania, it was originally made of water buffalo milk. Nowadays it is made throughout the peninsula, usually of cow's milk. It is widely used in cooking and also as a table cheese.

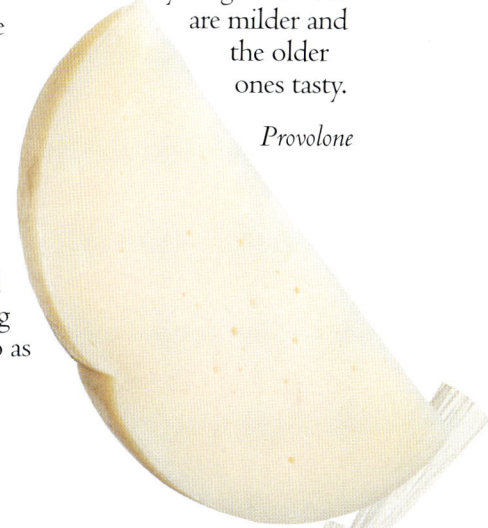

SCAMORZA
From Abruzzo and Molise in southern Italy, it is similar to mozzarella but harder and drier. It is recognisable by the shape it gets from being tied. The smoked variety has a much darker skin. Both a table and a cooking cheese.

PROVOLA
From Naples, provola is similar to scamorza in appearance and use. Also available as a smoked cheese.

Smoked scamorza

ASIAGO
Takes its name from a mountain area in the north, near Venice. There are two types; the aged variety is used in many regional dishes. The other, younger, variety is a table cheese.

FONTINA
This well-known cheese from the alpine Val d'Aosta, has an intense but sweet flavour. Many similar cheese are produced across northern Italy; they are usually called Fontal.

HERBS AND SPICES

These are precious ingredients. Many dishes owe their entire character to a particular herb or spice (or a combination of two or more). Most herbs can now be obtained fresh throughout the year in markets and greengrocers. The few seasonal varieties can be used in dry form. None of the spices here are rare or hard to find.

JUNIPER RRIES
Usually used in dry form to flavour food, juniper berries have a fragrant spicy aroma and a slightly bittersweet taste.

SAFFRON
Saffron is usually sold in powdered form. It is also available as threads which should be soaked in a little cold water for 30 minutes before use. A fairly expensive spice, it is normally used in very small quantities.

NUTMEG
Always buy nutmegs whole together with their little grater and grate as needed. Powdered nutmeg loses it flavour very quickly. Store the whole nutmegs in an airtight jar.

SAGE
Sage is used as leaves or twigs either whole or chopped. Fresh sage has a very strong and intense flavour. In its dried form it is blander and sweeter, but still good.

BAY LEAVES
Fresh bay leaves have a very intense flavour and should be used sparingly. The dried variety also produce excellent results.

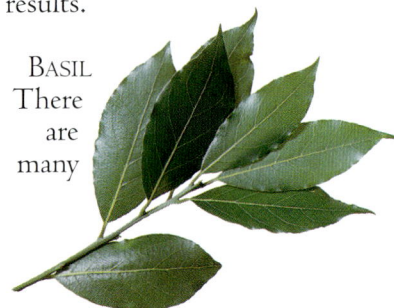

BASIL
There are many

CHILLIES
The many different types vary greatly in shape, size and spiciness. They can be used crushed, chopped or whole.

MINT
There are many varieties of mint, but the most commonly used ones in cookery are peppermint and spearmint. Best fresh, it can be used in dry form, but never powdered.

BLACK AND WHITE PEPPER CORNS
Black pepper is the whole seed of the pepper tree; the white variety is the same without its outer covering. Black pepper has a full, rounded flavour. White pepper is spicier and more pungent. Both should be ground just before use.

ROSEMARY
Whole twigs can be added to many dishes; sometimes the leaves are bound with cotton so that they won't get lost during cooking. The twig is removed and discarded at the end. Can also be used in finely chopped form.

GARLIC
Garlic can be used in a variety of ways, depending on how much of its distinctive flavour you want to include in a dish. It can be added whole, chopped, crushed or lightly bruised. Stored in a dry, well-aired place, it will keep for months.

ARUGULA (ROCKET)
This Mediterranean herb has been naturalised in many parts of the world. With its pungent, peppery flavour, it is widely used in salads and to flavour dishes.

FLAT-LEAF PARSLEY
This herb should always be used fresh since it is almost tasteless in its dried form. Fortunately, it is available fresh all year round. In Italy, this flat-leaf variety is the most common; if you can't get it, use ordinary curly-leaf parsley instead.

CELERY
An essential ingredient in sauces and broths, and widely used to flavour many soup and rice dishes. It has a distinctive, but not aggressive taste.

ONION
Used throughout the world in an almost endless number of ways. At least one of the many varieties is always available. Some of the recipes in this book require you to stick the onion with cloves as shown here.

BASIL
There are many different varieties, distinguished by the size of the leaves and the amount of flavour they carry. In most cases this herb should be torn rather than finely chopped.

OTHER INGREDIENTS

This is a selection of some of the other ingredients used in many of the recipes to follow. Most will be familiar and easy-to-find. The ones that aren't always available, such as porcini mushrooms, can be replaced with local varieties.

PRESERVED VEGETABLES
Many vegetables are preserved in pickles, brines or oil. Often served as appetisers, they are also an excellent way of enlivening many rice salads.

PORCINI MUSHROOMS
Four different types of porcini mushroom grow wild in the woods of Italy and are all much sought. Porcini are served raw in salads when young and firm to the touch. They can also be grilled, fried or made into many delicious sauces or toppings.

DRIED PORCINI MUSHROOMS
Although expensive, they are widely available. Soak a small quantity for 30 minutes in a bowl of warm water and mix with cultivated varieties to flavour sauces.

CAPERS
Capers are the unopened buds of a flowering plant that grows on Mediterranean hillsides. They are either packed in salt or pickled in vinegar. The pickled variety keeps well in the refrigerator.

BONE MARROW
This is the fatty substance from the inside of cattle bones. Once widely used, it is now limited to a number of regional dishes (such as *Osso buco* in Tuscany). It is considered a great delicacy by many.

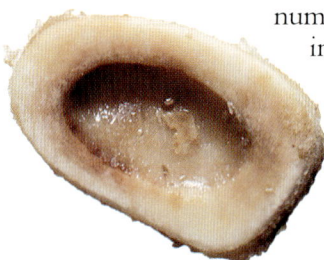

OLIVES
Olives are grown throughout the Mediterranean to produce oil. Processed in salt, they are widely used to flavour salads and other dishes.

SHRIMPS / PRAWNS

Shrimps are usually shelled and the heads cut off before serving. They are easier to shell after they have been cooked. They should always be extremely fresh; frozen ones are an acceptable substitute if they are not available fresh.

MOSCARDINE (TINY OCTOPUSES)

If you can't find these succulent little octopuses fresh or frozen, they can be replaced with small squid.

ANCHOVY FILLETS IN OLIVE OIL

A small quantity of crumbled anchovy fillets make a delicious addition to many dishes. They are also available cured in salt.

CUTTLEFISH

In Italy these tasty little ink squid are called *seppie*. They are used to flavour many dishes.

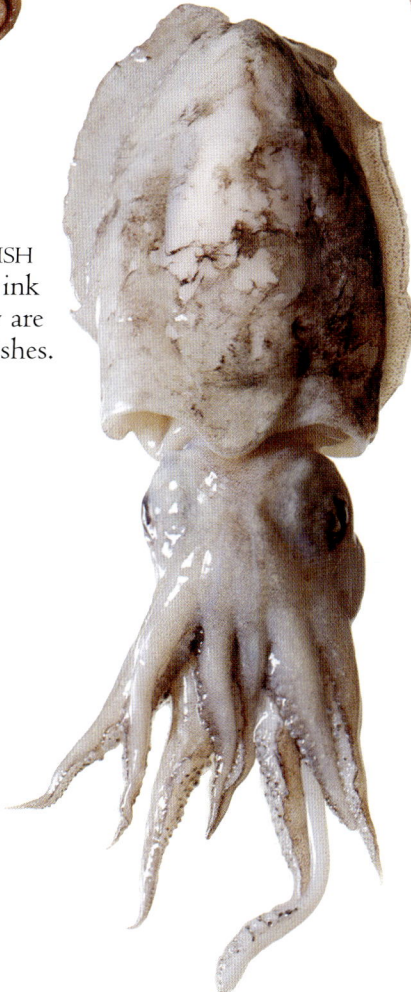

OLIVE OIL

Every cuisine is associated with a range of recurrent tastes and flavours. Olive oil plays a predominant role in Italian cookery. The quality of the oil can make or break a dish and ruin or exalt all your efforts. For this reason always buy Italian-made olive oil which is clearly labelled "*extra-vergine*". Make sure too that it is fresh; top quality new oil is a limpid green colour, not murky yellow.

BUTTER

Traditionally associated with French cuisine, some excellent butters are produced in northern Italy. Italian butter is almost always unsalted.

PORK PRODUCTS

Dating from harder times, in traditional cuisine little or nothing of the pig is wasted. The various parts are preserved and cured in a variety of ways and used to flavour and improve many soup, rice and polenta dishes. These are the pork products used in the following recipes. Some will not be readily found and in that case you should follow our suggestions for replacing them with similar products.

PANCETTA
Pancetta is made by curing pork slowly in a mixture of salt, pepper and spices. Usually unsmoked, some smoked varieties are available. When smoked it is very similar to bacon.

SPECK
This is a speciality of Alto Adige in northeastern Italy. It is made by curing pork in various spices and salt, then leaving it to age for 3 weeks. It is then smoked. If you can't get speck, use bacon in its place.

PROSCIUTTO
Produced throughout Italy, prosciutto is made by curing ham. The techniques are similar throughout the country, but the results vary greatly depending on the ability of the producers and also the climate and environmental conditions. Parma ham is generally considered the best, but there are some other excellent varieties available.

HAM
Italian ham is prepared in a similar way to English ham, by being flavoured by various spices then slowly cooked in vapour. Be sure to trim off and discard excess fat.

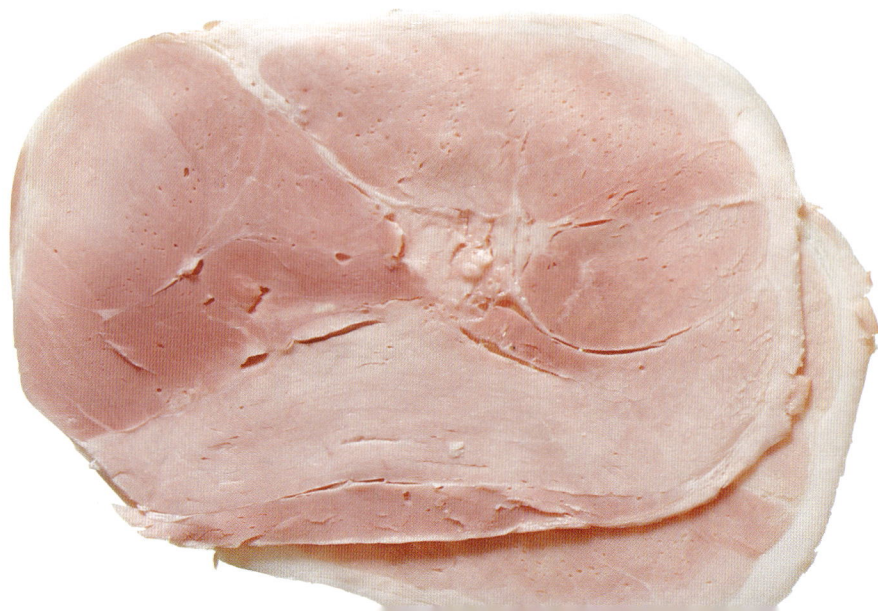

SAUSAGES

Every region, indeed every locality in Italy has its own special brand of spicy *salsicce*, or sausages. They are tastier than most English sausages. Nowadays they are not uncommon in supermarkets, butchers, and speciality shops.

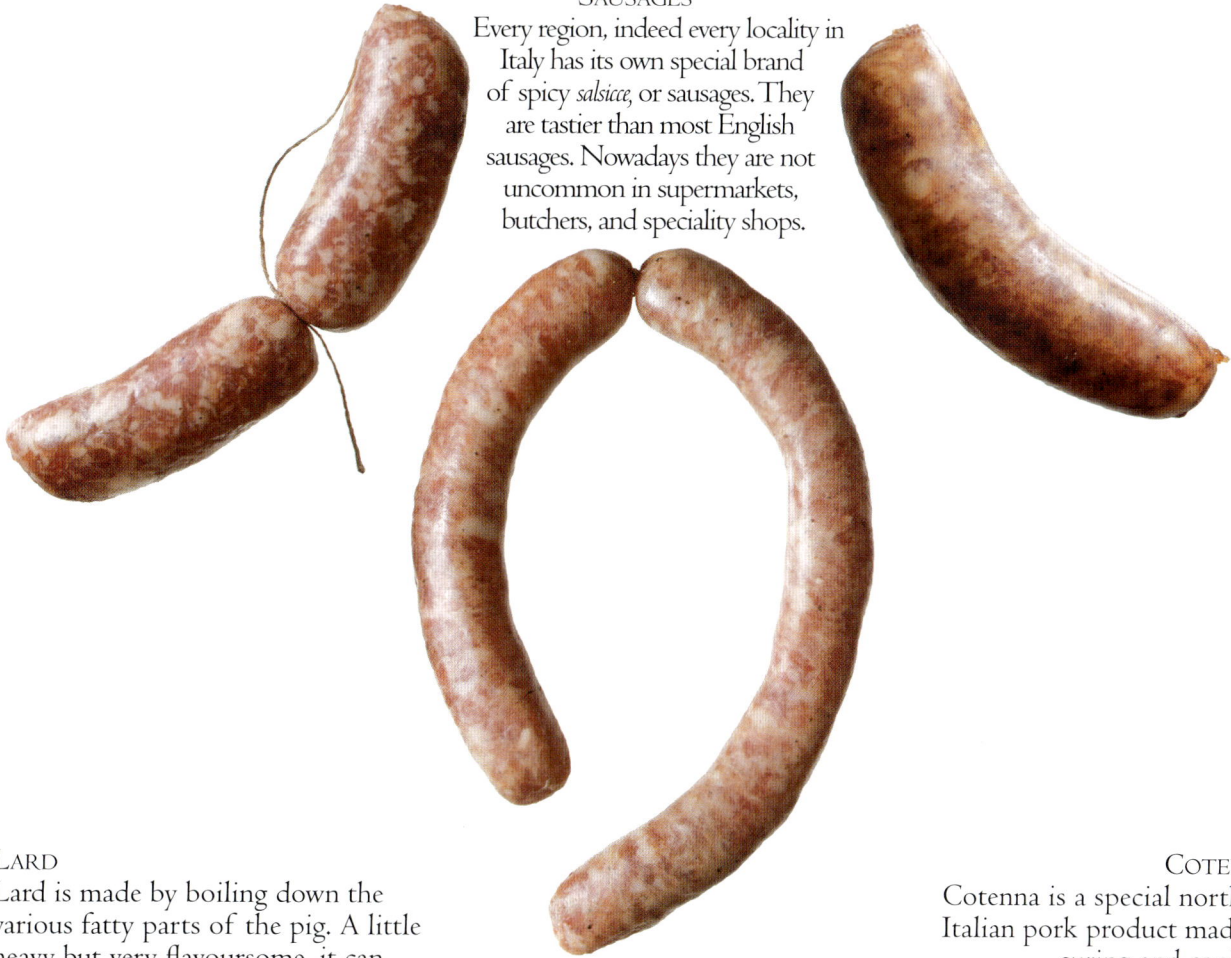

LARD

Lard is made by boiling down the various fatty parts of the pig. A little heavy but very flavoursome, it can be used to impart its distinctive, delicate taste to many soups and risottos. Use butter or oil if you prefer.

COTENNA

Cotenna is a special northern Italian pork product made by curing and cooking pigskin. Even in Italy it is only found during the winter months. If you can't find it in a speciality shop, use the same quantity of pancetta, or failing that, bacon.

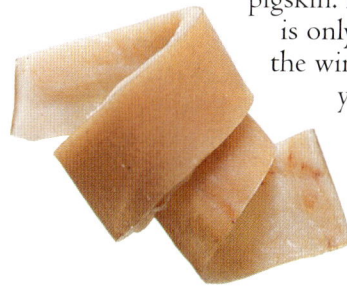

SALT PORK

This is the fatty part of the pig attached just under the skin. It is cured in salt and aged briefly. It is used to add taste to onion, garlic, and parsley mixtures when sautéed. Nowadays oil or butter are often used instead.

RICE, FLOUR, AND LEGUMES

It is very important to choose the correct type and quality of rice for the different dishes. Choose a plump, short-grain Italian rice for risotti—*Arborio* is the best choice, while *Vialone nano*, whose kernel offers some resistance to the bite, is ideal for rice salads. Brown rice is also very tasty in salads. Smaller, short-grain rices are generally used in soups.

ALMONDS

RAISINS

SEMOLINA

YELLOW COARSE-GRAIN
CORNMEAL / POLENTA

WHITE CORNMEAL

BUCK WHEAT
FLOUR

FINELY GROUND
YELLOW CORNMEAL

LENTILS

TOSCANELLI BEANS
(similar to white beans)

EMMER WHEAT

BROAD BEANS

WHITE BORLOTTI BEANS
(also available as a red bean, they are
similar to kidney beans)

CHICK PEAS

ARBORIO RICE
(good for risotto)

BROWN RICE

RICE FOR SOUPS

BASIC RECIPES

POLENTA
Basic polenta

This is the basic recipe for a firm polenta. When transferred to a cutting board or platter, it will keep its shape.

■ INGREDIENTS

- 2 litres (2 quarts) water
- 1 heaped tablespoon coarse sea salt
- 450 g (14 oz) coarse-grain cornmeal

Serves 4; Preparation: 5 minutes; Cooking: 50-60 minutes; Level of difficulty: Medium

Bring the salted water to a boil in a heavy-bottomed pot large enough to hold 5 litres (5 quarts). § Add the cornmeal gradually, stirring continuously and rapidly with a whisk so that no lumps form; polenta should always be perfectly smooth. § To cook, stir the polenta over high heat by moving a long wooden spoon in a circular motion. At a certain point you'll notice that it begins to withdraw from the sides of the pot on which a thin crust is forming. § The polenta should be stirred almost continuously for the 50-60 minutes it takes to cook. § Quantities and method are the same when using an electric polenta cauldron. Stir the cornmeal into the boiling water gradually, then turn on the mixer. Leave for 50-60 minutes. § Serve hot or cold as suggested in the recipes.

POLENTA BIANCA
White polenta

This polenta, typical of Veneto and Friuli in the northeast, is made with white cornmeal in exactly the same way as yellow cornmeal polenta. Proportionally more water is used and the white polenta is a little softer than the yellow.

■ INGREDIENTS

- 2 litres (2 quarts) water
- 1 heaped tablespoon coarse sea salt
- 350 g (11 oz) white cornmeal

Serves 4; Preparation: 5 minutes; Cooking: 50-60 minutes; Level of difficulty: Medium

Prepare the polenta as explained above. § When ready, spread out on a cutting board to a thickness of about 5 cm (2 in), cover with a damp cloth, and let cool. § Cut into slices about 12 mm (½-in) thick and roast on a charcoal grill or in a sizzling grill pan. § The slices can also be fried in oil or lard. § Serve hot or cold.

Right: *Polenta*

RAGÙ AL POMODORO
Tomato meat sauce

There are many different recipes for ragù. Most require fairly long cooking to reach their full flavour. This tomato ragù goes very well with any pasta, but it is also perfect for simple or baked polenta (prepared with alternating layers of béchamel and grated or flaked cheese).

Serves 4; Preparation: 10 minutes; Cooking: 2 hours; Level of difficulty: Simple

Melt the butter in a heavy-bottomed saucepan until it bubbles. Add the pancetta, onion, carrot and celery and sauté over low heat for 10 minutes, stirring often. § Add the pork and veal or beef and cook for 5 minutes more, mixing well. § Add half the wine and, when it has partially evaporated, add a third of the stock. § Simmer until the liquid has reduced, then add the tomato paste and a little more wine and stock. § After 10-15 minutes, add the tomatoes, salt and pepper. § Continue cooking over low heat, gradually stirring in the remaining wine and stock. When cooked, the sauce should be fairly thick. This will take about 2 hours in all.

VARIATION
– Add a pinch of nutmeg just before removing from the heat.

■ INGREDIENTS

- 2 tablespoons butter
- 60 g (2 oz) diced pancetta
- 1 small onion, 1 small carrot, 1 stalk celery, finely chopped
- 150 g (5 oz) lean minced pork
- 100 g (3½ oz) minced veal or beef
- 250 ml (1 cup) red wine
- 250 ml (1 cup) boiling beef stock (see recipe p. 24)
- 1 tablespoon tomato paste
- 250 g (1 cup) peeled and chopped canned tomatoes
- salt and freshly ground black pepper

INTINGOLO DI FEGATINI
Chicken liver sauce

This sauce is very good with polenta and with all egg-based pasta types. It can also be served on simple boiled rice. It is particularly good with Risotto bianco al parmigiano (see recipe p. 79). Prepare the risotto and press it into a ring mould pan. Invert immediately onto a serving dish and spoon the chicken liver sauce over the top. Serve hot.

Serves 4; Preparation: 15 minutes; Cooking: 30 minutess; Level of difficulty: Simple

Heat the oil in a small frying pan and sauté the onion, carrot and celery over medium-low heat for 6-7 minutes. § Add the chicken livers and cook for 2-3 minutes. § Pour in the wine and after another 2-3 mintes, add the tomato paste diluted in 200 ml (scant 1 cup) of water. Mix well, and add the peas. § Cook for another 15-20 minutes. § Serve hot as suggested above.

■ INGREDIENTS

- 5 tablespoons extra-virgin olive oil
- 1 small onion, 1 small carrot, 1 stalk celery, finely chopped
- 6 chicken livers, cleaned and coarsely chopped
- 3 tablespoons dry red or white wine
- 1 tablespoon tomato paste
- 100 g (3½ oz) shelled peas
- salt and freshly ground white pepper

Right: Polenta con ragù di pomodoro

Ragù di salsiccia
Italian sausage sauce

This recipe, based on Italian sausage meat, is one of the few meat sauces that doesn't require hours to cook.

Serves 4; Preparation: 5 minutes; Cooking: 30 minutes; Level of difficulty: Simple

Melt the butter in a small saucepan. § Add the sausage and the bay leaf and sauté over medium-low heat for 5 minutes. § Pour in the wine and let it reduce by about a half. § Add the tomatoes with their juice and mash a little with a fork. § Cook over medium heat, stirring occasionally, for about 20 minutes. § Taste before seasoning with salt and pepper; the sausages are often very spicy and salty and the sauce may not require any extra seasoning. § Remove the bay leaf just before serving.

■ INGREDIENTS

- 2 tablespoons butter
- 300 g (10 oz) Italian pork sausage, peeled and crumbled
- 1 bay leaf
- 125 ml (½ cup) dry white or red wine
- 300 g (10 oz) peeled and chopped canned tomatoes
- salt and freshly ground black pepper

Ragù bianco
Meat sauce

Serves 4; Preparation: 10 minutes; Cooking: 2 hours; Level of difficulty: Simple

Follow the recipe for the *Tomato meat sauce* on p. 18 until the meat is well-browned and seasoned with the onion, carrot and celery. § Add the milk and simmer over low heat for 1 hour, stirring occasionally. § Add the anchovies and capers. Cook for another 30 minutes, adding more milk if the sauce becomes too dry. § When cooked, the sauce should be rather thick. Season with salt and pepper.

■ INGREDIENTS

- 2 tablespoons butter
- 60 g (2 oz) diced pancetta
- 1 medium onion, 1 small carrot, 1 small celery stalk, finely chopped
- 150 g (5 oz) lean beef, coarsely chopped
- 100 g (3½ oz) lean pork, coarsely chopped
- 1 tablespoon tomato paste
- 500 ml (2 cups) hot milk
- 1 anchovy fillet, crumbled
- 1 teaspoon capers, finely chopped
- salt and black pepper

Salsa besciamella
Béchamel sauce

Serves 4; Preparation: 5 minutes; Cooking: 10 minutes; Level of difficulty: Simple

Heat the milk in a saucepan until it is almost boiling. § In a heavy-bottomed saucepan, melt the butter with the flour over low heat, stirring rapidly with a wooden spoon. Cook for about 1 minute. § Remove from heat and add half the hot milk, stirring constantly. Return to low heat and stir until the sauce starts to thicken. § Add the rest of the milk gradually and continue stirring until it comes to a boil. § Season with salt to taste and continue stirring until the béchamel is the right thickness. § If any lumps form, beat the sauce rapidly with a fork or whisk until they dissolve.

■ INGREDIENTS

- 500 ml (2 cups) milk
- 60 g (2 oz) butter
- 60 g (2 oz) white flour
- salt

Right: *Preparing béchamel sauce*

SALSA DI POMODORO
Basic tomato sauce

Serves 4; Preparation: 5 minutes; Cooking: 25-30 minutes; Level of difficulty: Simple

Combine the tomatoes (with their liquid), onion, garlic and parsley in a small heavy-bottomed saucepan. § Bring to a boil over high heat, then lower the heat and partially cover with a lid. Simmer for 20 minutes checking occasionally that there is enough liquid. If the sauce becomes too dry add a little water and cover completely so that it doesn't dry out. § Press the sauce through a sieve to strain. § Add the basil, salt and pepper, and simmer for another 5 minutes. § Add the oil just before removing from the heat. The uncooked oil will give its own special flavour to the sauce.

■ INGREDIENTS

- 450 g (14 oz) canned tomatoes
- 1 medium onion
- 1 clove garlic, finely chopped
- 2 tablespoons finely chopped parsley
- salt and freshly ground black or white pepper
- 7 leaves fresh basil, torn
- 4 tablespoons extra-virgin olive oil

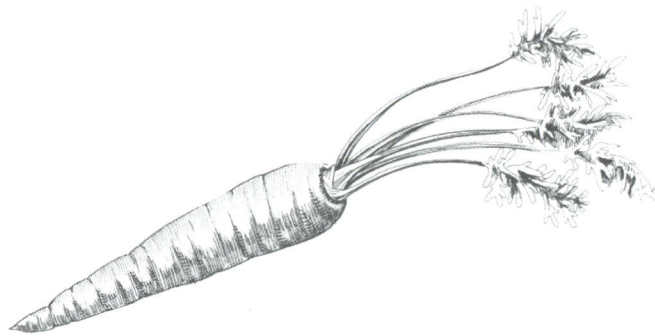

BRODO DI VERDURE
Vegetable stock

Vegetable stock is an essential ingredient in many soups and risotti. Vegetarians can use it in recipes that call for chicken or beef stock. For a completely fat-free stock, omit the butter and put all the ingredients together in 2 litres (2 quarts) of lightly salted water, and simmer for about an hour.

Makes about 1.5 litres (1½ quarts); Preparation: 15 minutes; Cooking: 1¼ hours; Level of difficulty: Simple

Melt the butter in a fairly large pot and add the vegetables. Cover and simmer over low heat for 10 minutes, stirring occasionally. § Add the parsley, peppercorns, cloves, and bay leaf. § Add 2 litres (2 quarts) of water, season lightly with salt, and simmer for 1 hour over low heat, skimming off the foam occasionally. § Strain the stock, discarding the vegetables.

■ INGREDIENTS

- 2 tablespoons butter
- 1 medium onion, 1 carrot, 1 medium leek, 2 celery stalks, with leaves, all cleaned and cut in 4 pieces
- 1 small tomato, cut in half (optional)
- 6 sprigs parsley
- 4 black peppercorns
- 1 clove
- ½ bay leaf (optional)
- salt

Right: *Salsa di pomodoro*

Brodo di carne
Beef stock

Nowadays stock is often made with a bouillon cube and boiling water. Although simpler and quite satisfactory tastewise, some soups really require an authentic meat stock base to be perfect. Making stock is time consuming, so it is advisable to make a lot. You may even want to double the quantities given here. Stock freezes well; pour it into the ice cube tray and take it out as you need it.

Makes about 3 litres (3 quarts); Preparation: 15 minutes; Cooking: 3 hours; Level of difficulty: Simple

Rinse the bones quickly under cold running water. § Put the meat and bones in a pot that will hold about 9 litres (9 quarts). Add the celery, carrots, onion, garlic, pepper corns (or crushed chillies) and juniper berries. § Add a generous 4 litres (4 quarts) of cold water and simmer over medium-low heat for 3 hours. Skim off the surface foam occasionally with a slotted spoon. § When ready, taste for salt. Strain the stock, discarding the vegetables, seasoning and bones. § The meat can be used for meat balls, meat loaf or salads. § To remove extra fat, let the stock cool and then refrigerate for about 2 hours. The fat will solidify on top and can easily be lifted off.

■ INGREDIENTS

- 1 kg (2 lb) (or more) beef with bones (neck, shoulder, short ribs, brisket, various cuts of lean meat)
- 1 spongy bone (knee)
- 1 small piece ox-bone marrow (optional)
- 2 celery stalks, with leaves, washed and broken into 2-3 pieces
- 2 medium carrots, scraped and cut in half
- 1 large onion, stuck with 3-4 cloves
- 2 cloves garlic
- 6 black pepper corns (or ¼ teaspoon crushed dried chillies)
- 3 juniper berries
- salt

Brodo di pollo
Chicken stock

The tastiest chicken stock is made with free-range chickens; unfortunately they are not easy to find nowadays. Soup chickens do still exist however, even if battery-raised. Once again, it pays to make a large amount of stock and freeze it in small quantities to be used as needed.

Makes about 3 litres (3 quarts); Preparation: 10 minutes; Cooking: 3 hours; Level of difficulty: Simple

Put the chicken, whole, in a very large pot. Add the celery, carrots, onion and peppercorns. Cover with about 5 litres (5 quarts) of cold water and simmer for 3 hours over medium-low heat. The water should barely move. § Strain the stock, discarding the vegetables. The chicken can be served hot or cold with a favourite sauce, or in chicken aspic or salad. § To remove the fat, in part or completely, let the stock cool, then refrigerate for about 2 hours. The fat will solidify on the top and can easily be lifted off.

■ INGREDIENTS

- 1 chicken, cleaned, about 2 kg (4 lb)
- 2 celery stalks, with leaves, washed and broken into 3 pieces
- 2 medium carrots, scraped and cut in half
- 1 large onion, stuck with 2 cloves (optional)
- 4 black pepper corns
- salt

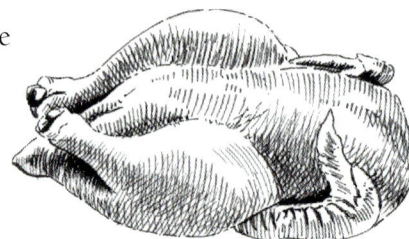

Right: *Brodo di pollo*

Soups

Soups are more typical of the northern and central regions of Italy. They range from simple broths and delicate creams, to rustic minestrone and other hearty soups, often prepared with bread, rice or pasta.

Minestrone alla milanese
Milanese-style minestrone

Traditional Milanese minestrone contains cotenna and rice rather than pasta. If you can't find cotenna, double the quantity of pancetta. Traditionally, minestrone was simmered for 6 hours; there is a tendency to cut down on cooking time nowadays.

Serves 4; Preparation: 30 minutes; Cooking: 2 hours; Level of difficulty: Medium

Put the cotenna, pancetta, garlic, onion, celery, parsley, sage, rosemary, potato, carrots, courgettes, tomatoes and beans in a large pot. Add 2 litres (2 quarts) boiling water, cover and simmer over low heat for at least 1¼ hours. § Chop the cabbage in 1.5 cm (¾-in) strips and add with the peas. Cook for another 25 minutes. § Season with salt and pepper and add the rice. § The minestrone will be cooked in about 20 minutes. § Serve with the parmesan passed separately.

VARIATIONS
– Add 2 leaves of finely chopped sage.
– If you want a simple but very special vegetable soup, omit the rice.

■ INGREDIENTS

- 150 g (5 oz) cotenna, scraped and cut in 6 mm (¼-in) strips
- 90 g (3 oz) diced pancetta
- 1 clove garlic, finely chopped
- 1 onion, coarsely chopped
- 2 celery stalks, sliced
- 1 tablespoon coarsely chopped parsley
- fresh rosemary leaves
- 1 potato, 2 carrots, 2 courgettes (zucchini), 2 tomatoes, diced
- 150 g (5 oz) red kidney beans
- 90 g (3 oz) shelled peas
- ½ small Savoy cabbage
- 150 g (5 oz) rice
- salt and freshly ground black pepper
- 4 tablespoons freshly grated parmesan cheese

Wine: a light, dry red (Riviera del Garda Bresciano - Chiaretto)

Minestrone di Asti
Asti-style minestrone

Serves 4; Preparation: 20 minutes; Cooking: 1¼ hours; Level of difficulty: Simple

Put the beans in a large pot and cover with cold water to about 5 cm (2 in) above the top of the beans. § Cover and simmer over low heat for about 30 minutes. § Cut the cabbage in 6 mm (¼-in) thick strips, discarding the core. § Add the cabbage, potatoes, carrots and celery to the pot, stir, and cook for 30 minutes more. § If needed, add a little boiling water, although the soup should be quite thick. § Add the rice and, after 15 minutes, the lard, garlic, parsley and basil. Stir well. § Taste for salt and pepper. § Turn off heat and let the minestrone stand for a few minutes while the rice finishes cooking. § Serve with the parmesan passed separately.

■ INGREDIENTS

- 250 g (8 oz) fresh cranberry or red kidney beans
- ½ small Savoy cabbage
- 2 medium potatoes, 2 small carrots, diced
- 2 celery stalks, sliced
- 200 g (6½ oz) rice
- 60 g (2 oz) lard, 1 clove garlic, 1 tablespoon parsley, 1 tablespoon basil, all finely chopped
- salt and freshly ground black pepper
- 4 tablespoons freshly grated parmesan cheese

Wine: a dry red (Dolcetto d'Asti)

Right: *Minestrone alla milanese*

ZUPPA ALLA PAVESE
Pavia soup

According to tradition, on February 24, 1525, Francis I of France, at war with Charles V of Spain, near Pavia (northern Italy), felt pangs of hunger after a long day on the battlefield. A peasant woman in a nearby farmhouse made him a soup with the only ingredients she had: millet bread, fresh eggs and bean stock. Francis I lost the war but Zuppa alla pavese, with a few changes, is still a winner.

Serves 4; Preparation: 10 minutes; Cooking: 5 minutes; Level of difficulty: Simple

Fry the slices of bread, on both sides, in the butter. You will probably not be able to fry them all at once unless you have a really large frying pan, so melt half the butter and, when it no longer foams, arrange half the slices in the frying pan, turning them when the underside is golden. Repeat the procedure. The bread must be golden and crisp but be careful not to burn it. § Place two slices in preheated, individual soup bowls. § Break one or two eggs carefully over the toast, making sure that the yolks remain whole. § Sprinkle with the parmesan and dust with pepper. Pour some of the stock into each bowl, taking care not to pour it directly onto the eggs. § Let stand for a minute, then serve.

■ INGREDIENTS

- 3 tablespoons butter
- 8 slices of firm, densely-textured bread, about 2 cm (¾-in) thick
- 4-8 fresh eggs
- 4 tablespoons of freshly grated parmesan cheese
- freshly ground white pepper
- 1 litre (1 quart) boiling beef or chicken stock (see recipes p. 24)

Wine: a dry, fragrant white (Pinot Bianco Oltrepò Pavese)

MINESTRA DI RISO E PREZZEMOLO
Rice and parsley soup

Many traditional recipes from Lombardy are based on rice. They are all simple, light and fragrant.

Serves 4; Preparation: 5 minutes; Cooking: 20 minutes; Level of difficulty: Simple

Bring the stock to a boil and add the rice. § Simmer for about 15 minutes. § Just before removing from the heat, add the parsley, butter and, if liked, the sage. Taste for salt and serve immediately. Garnish with the parmesan.

VARIATION
– For a richer dish, put an egg in the tureen and whisk together with 2 tablespoons parmesan. Pour in the soup, stirring quickly with the whisk.

■ INGREDIENTS

- 1.2 litres (5 cups) beef stock (see recipe p. 24)
- 200 g (6½ oz) rice
- 1 tablespoon finely chopped fresh parsley
- ½ fresh sage leaf, finely chopped (optional)
- salt
- 1 tablespoon butter
- 4 tablespoons freshly grated parmesan cheese

Wine: a dry white (Breganze Vespaiolo)

Right: *Minestra di riso e prezzemolo*

- 1 carrot, 1 medium turnip, 1 courgette (zucchini), 1 large potato, all cleaned and diced
- 1 leek (white part only), 2 small celery hearts, cleaned and sliced
- 1 medium onion, 30 g (1 oz) spinach, cleaned and coarsely chopped
- 1 tablespoon finely chopped parsley
- 90 g (3 oz) diced smoked pancetta
- 1.5 litres (1½ quarts) boiling beef stock (see recipe p. 24)
- 200 g (6½ oz) brown barley
- salt and freshly ground black pepper
- 3-4 tablespoons extra-virgin olive oil

Wine: a dry rosè (Casteller)

- 2 tablespoons butter
- 1 medium potato, diced
- 2 small leeks, cleaned and sliced (white part only)
- 150 g (5 oz) spinach, coarsely chopped
- 1.2 litres (5 cups) boiling beef stock (see recipe p. 24)
- 150 g (5 oz) rice
- salt
- 4 tablespoons freshly grated parmesan cheese

Wine: a dry white (Tocai di Lison)

Left: Orzetto alla Trentina

ORZETTO ALLA TRENTINA
Trento-style barley soup

Some versions of this delicious soup use pearl barley. I prefer to use unrefined brown barley, which differs in flavour and consistency. If you are unable to find it, use pearl barley. It will take about 30 minutes less to cook.

Serves 4; Preparation: 30 minutes; Cooking: 1½ hours; Level of difficulty: Simple

Put all the vegetables and the pancetta in a large pot. Add the stock and when it begins to boil, add the barley (previously rinsed by putting it in a colander and passing it under cold running water). Cover the pot, and simmer for 1½ hours, stirring occasionally. § Season with salt and pepper and add the oil. Alternatively, pass the oil separately to be added at the table.

MINESTRA DI RISO E VERDURE
Rice and vegetable soup

There are many light and tasty soups in Milanese cuisine. They are usually served for the evening meal.

Serves 4; Preparation: 20 minutes; Cooking: 30 minutes; Level of difficulty: Simple

Melt the butter in a saucepan over low heat and add the potato, leeks and spinach. Sauté for a couple of minutes, stirring continuously. § Add the stock and simmer, covered, for 10 or more minutes. § Add the rice and stir. § The rice will be cooked in about 15 minutes. Taste for salt and sprinkle with the parmesan.

VARIATION
— Use the same quantity of young Swiss chard (silver beet) instead of spinach.

RISO E LATTE
Rice and milk

A favourite with children, Zuppe di riso e latte is an exquisite, rather thick soup. Served with a glass of cool, dry white wine, adults will also appreciate its delicate flavours.

Serves 4; Preparation: 5 minutes; Cooking: 35 minutes; Level of difficulty: Simple

Put the milk and water in a saucepan with ½ teaspoon salt and bring to a boil over high heat. § Add the rice and stir. Reduce the heat and cook for 25 minutes. The amount of cooking time depends on the quality of the rice, so taste it after about 25 minutes to see if it is ready. It should be *al dente* (slightly firm, but cooked). Add more salt if necessary. § Turn off the heat and add the butter. § Cover and let the soup stand for a few minutes. Serve hot with a bowl of parmesan passed separately at table.

■ INGREDIENTS

- 1.5 litres (1½ quarts) whole milk
- 250 ml (1 cup) water
- 200 g (6½ oz) small-grain rice
- salt
- 1½ tablespoons butter
- freshly grated parmesan cheese

Wine: a light, dry white (Gambellara)

CREMA DI PISELLI
Cream of pea soup

Serves 4; Preparation: 10 minutes; Cooking: 20-25 minutes; Level of difficulty: Simple

Melt the butter in a saucepan over low heat. Add the onion and sauté until it is soft and translucent. § Stir in the peas and cook for a minute or two. § Add 750 ml (3 cups) of the stock and cook for about 20 minutes. § In the meantime, make the béchamel sauce and set aside. § When the peas are cooked, press them through a strainer, or use a blender or an electric hand mixer to make them into a smooth, fairly liquid purée. § Incorporate the béchamel sauce and mix thoroughly. If the soup seems too dense, add some of the remaining stock. Taste for salt. § Return the pan to medium heat for 2-3 minutes until the soup is hot enough to be served.

■ INGREDIENTS

- 2½ tablespoons butter
- 1 small onion, finely chopped
- 450 g (14 oz) shelled fresh peas
- 1 litre (1 quart) boiling beef stock (see recipe   p. 24)
- salt
- 1 quantity béchamel sauce (see recipe p. 24)

Wine: a dry white (Pinot Grigio Grave del Friuli)

VARIATIONS
– Use the same quantity of frozen peas instead of fresh ones.
– For a richer dish, dice 2 slices of day-old bread into 12 mm (½-in) cubes and fry in 2 tablespoons of butter until golden brown. Sprinkle over the soup just before serving.

Right:
Crema di piselli

INGREDIENTS

- 1 large celery plant
- juice of 1 lemon
- salt and freshly ground black pepper
- 1 tablespoon butter
- 1 tablespoon white wine
- 1 tablespoon parsley and 1 clove garlic, finely chopped
- 250 ml (1 cup) vegetable stock (see recipe p. 22)

Wine: a dry white (Frascati)

CREMA DI SEDANO
Cream of celery soup

Serves 4; Preparation: 15 minutes; Cooking: 20 minutes; Level of difficulty: Simple

Clean the celery and remove any tough outer stalks and stringy fibres. Chop coarsely and soak in a bowl of water with the lemon juice for 10 minutes. § Cook the celery in a pot of salted, boiling water for 5 minutes. Drain well. § Transfer to a heavy-bottomed pan and add the butter, wine, parsley, garlic, salt and pepper. Cook until the wine evaporates. § Add the stock and simmer for 10-15 minutes more. § Purée in a food mill. Return to the heat for 2-3 minutes. § Serve hot.

ZUPPA DI LENTICCHIE
Lentil soup

*The amount of cooking time will vary depending on the age and quality of the lentils used.
If they are not soft after 50 minutes, add a little boiling water and continue cooking until they are.*

Serves 4; Preparation: 10 minutes + 3 hours for soaking lentils; Cooking: 50 minutes; Level of difficulty: Simple

Put the lentils in a bowl and add cold water to cover by about 3 cm (1¼ in). Let soak for 3 hours. § Drain the lentils and place in a saucepan with the onion, carrots, celery, bay leaf and garlic. Add enough cold water to cover to about 5 cm (2 in) above the level of the lentils. § Cover and cook over low heat for about 45 minutes. § Discard the bay leaf, add the sage and rosemary and continue cooking, still covered and over low heat, for another 5-10 minutes or so. § At this point the lentils should be very soft and will begin to disintegrate. Add salt and pepper to taste, drizzle with the oil, and serve hot.

VARIATION
— To make cream of lentil soup, press the cooked lentils through a strainer, or purée in a processor or with an electric hand mixer. Sprinkle with 1 tablespoon of finely chopped parsley just before serving.

ZUPPA DI BROCCOLO ROMANESCO
Green Roman cauliflower soup

This type of cauliflower is a beautiful emerald green and the florets are pointed rather than rounded as in white cauliflower. It is typical of Latium, the region around Rome. If you can't find it in your local market, use green sprouting broccoli in its place.

Serves 4; Preparation: 10 minutes; Cooking: 10 minutes; Level of difficulty: Simple

Separate the florets from the core of the cauliflower, keeping the tender inner leaves. Rinse thoroughly and place in a pot of salted, boiling water. Cook for about 8-10 minutes. § In the meantime, toast the bread, rub the slices with the garlic and place them in individual soup bowls. When the cauliflower is cooked, pour several tablespoons of the cooking water over each slice. § Arrange the florets and leaves, well drained, on the toasted bread. Drizzle with the oil and lemon juice, and add salt and pepper to taste. § Serve immediately.

■ INGREDIENTS

- 300 g (10 oz) dried lentils
- 1 medium onion, finely chopped
- 2 small carrots, scraped and diced
- 2 celery stalks, cleaned and thinly sliced
- 1 bay leaf
- 2 cloves garlic, whole or finely chopped (optional)
- 3 fresh sage leaves, finely chopped
- 1 heaped tablespoon finely chopped fresh rosemary leaves
- salt and freshly ground white or black pepper
- 4 tablespoons extra-virgin olive oil

Wine: a dry white (Verdicchio dei Castelli di Jesi)

■ INGREDIENTS

- 1 green Roman cauliflower, weighing about 1 kg (2 lb)
- 4 slices home-style bread
- 1 large clove garlic
- 6 tablespoons extra-virgin olive oil
- 1 tablespoon lemon juice
- salt and freshly ground white or black pepper

Wine: a flavourful white (Marino)

Right:
Zuppa di lenticchie

CREMA DI ZUCCA
Cream of squash

INGREDIENTS

- 1 kg (2 lb) yellow squash (hubbard or pumpkin) peeled and cut in pieces
- 300 g (10 oz) carrots, scraped and cut in pieces
- 300 g (10 oz) leeks, cleaned and cut in pieces (white part only)
- 3 small celery stalks, from the heart, cut in pieces
- 2 cloves garlic (optional)
- 1 litre (1 quart) boiling beef stock (see recipe p. 24)
- 125 ml (½ cup) light cream
- salt and freshly ground white pepper
- 6 tablespoons freshly grated parmesan cheese

Wine: a light red (Bardolino)

Serves 4; Preparation: 30 minutes; Cooking: 30 minutes; Level of difficulty: Simple

Put all the vegetables in a pot and add the stock, reserving a quarter. Cover and simmer for 25 minutes, stirring occasionally. If necessary, add more stock, a little at a time. § Press through a strainer or use a blender or an electric hand mixer to obtain a smooth, not too liquid purée. § Set over medium heat for 1-2 minutes. § Stir in the cream and add salt and pepper. § Let stand for a minute, sprinkle with the parmesan, and serve hot.

VARIATIONS
– Replace the leeks with the same quantity of onions.
– For a richer dish, dice 2 slices of day-old bread into 12 mm (½-in) cubes and fry in 2 tablespoons of butter until golden brown. Sprinkle over the soup just before serving.

SEMOLINO IN BRODO
Semolina in beef stock

INGREDIENTS

- 1.2 litres (5 cups) boiling beef stock (see recipe p. 28)
- 90 g (3 oz) coarse-grain semolina
- salt
- 1½ tablespoons butter
- freshly grated parmesan cheese

Wine: a light white (Colli Euganei Bianco)

Serves 4; Preparation: 5 minutes; Cooking: 20 minutes; Level of difficulty: Simple

Sift the semolina slowly into the boiling stock, over medium heat, stirring with a wire whisk so no lumps will form. § Simmer for 20 minutes, stirring occasionally. § Taste for salt. § One minute before serving, add the butter and stir one last time. § Serve with a bowl of freshly grated parmesan passed separately.

VARIATIONS
– Mix 1-2 egg yolks with 2 tablespoons of melted butter (omit the 1½ tablespoons butter added to the soup at the last minute) with the 3 tablespoons of parmesan and a pinch of nutmeg in the tureen. Dilute with half a ladle of the stock, stir rapidly with a whisk, and then slowly pour in the rest of the soup. Wait 1 minute before serving.
– Toasted bread cubes fried in butter always make a tasty garnish.

Left:
Crema di zucca

ZUPPA DI FARRO
Spelt soup

Spelt has been grown in Italy for thousands of years. It was a staple crop throughout the peninsula and was served as a sort of polenta or porridge. It was gradually replaced by strains of wheat from Egypt, although it is still grown, mainly in central Italy. It has become popular again in recent years as healthier eating habits have gained popularity. Look for it in speciality shops, or replace it with equal quantities of pearl barley.

Serves 4; Preparation: 20 minutes + 4 hours for soaking emmer wheat; Cooking: 1¾ hours; Level of difficulty: Simple

Put the spelt in a bowl and add enough cold water to cover by at least 5 cm (2 in). Leave to soak for 4 hours. § Put the beans in a saucepan with the sage and enough cold water to cover by 5 cm (2 in). Cover, and simmer for 45 minutes. § Discard the sage. Press half the beans through a strainer (or use a blender), with as much of the cooking water as needed to make a fairly dense cream. Then add the rest of the beans. § When only 20 minutes of the spelt's soaking time remain, combine the pancetta, leek, celery, carrot, Swiss chard, chillies and garlic in a saucepan. § Add the stock, bring to a boil, and cook over medium heat for 15 minutes. § Add the spelt, well drained, and half the oil and continue cooking for 20 minutes. § Add the beans and cook for another 20 minutes. § Season with salt, pepper and a pinch of nutmeg, if liked. § Drizzle with the remaining oil just before serving. § Serve hot.

VARIATIONS
— Fresh beans are only available for a few months of the year. If using dry beans in their place, allow an extra 10-12 hours soaking time in cold water and 2½ hours cooking time.
— Tinned beans are a quick and convenient solution. Use 450 g (14 oz) canned beans. They won't require preparatory cooking; just drain and press half of them directly through the strainer (or whisk in the blender) and continue as in the recipe.

Right: Zuppa di farro

Stracciatella
Rag soup

The name comes from the fact that when the eggs are rapidly mixed into the stock, they form strands or tatters, or in other words "rags". Versions differ slightly from one region to the next. This Roman recipe is perhaps the most classic.

Serves 4; Preparation: 2 minutes; Cooking: 1-2 minutes; Level of difficulty: Simple

Put the eggs, parmesan, a pinch of freshly grated nutmeg, salt and pepper in a bowl. § Whisk for a minute, until the mixture is well combined but not foamy. § Pour it into a pot containing the stock, over medium heat, and mix rapidly with the whisk. As soon as the stock begins to boil again, the soup is ready and should be served immediately.

VARIATIONS
– Add 1 tablespoon of chopped parsley to the egg mixture.
– Add 1 tablespoon of lemon juice to the soup just before serving.

■ INGREDIENTS

- 4 eggs
- 4 tablespoons freshly grated parmesan cheese
- pinch of nutmeg
- salt and freshly ground white pepper
- 1.2 litres (5 cups) boiling beef or chicken stock (see recipes p. 24)

Wine: a lightly sweet white (Bianco Capena)

Acquacotta
Cooked water

This soup was originally prepared with water, a few herbs, oil, eggs and stale bread. It was a staple in the diet of the butteri or cowboys of the Tuscan Maremma. It has become much richer over the years and there are many different versions. This is my favourite.

Serves 4; Preparation: 15 minutes; Cooking: 45 minutes; Level of difficulty: Medium

Plunge the tomatoes into boiling water for 10 seconds, then into cold water. Slip off the skins and cut them in half horizontally. Squeeze out some of the seeds and cut the flesh in pieces. § Heat the oil in a large pot, add the onions and sauté over medium heat, stirring frequently, until they are soft and translucent. § Add the tomatoes, celery and basil, and cook for 20 minutes. The sauce should be fairly thick. § Season with salt and pepper, add the water or stock and continue cooking for 20 minutes. § Lower the heat to the minimum. Break the eggs carefully into the soup, not too close together and taking care not to break the yolks. After 2-3

■ INGREDIENTS

- 450 g (14 oz) ripe tomatoes
- 2 onions, sliced
- 4-5 tablespoons extra-virgin olive oil
- 2 celery stalks, cleaned and finely chopped
- 10 fresh basil leaves
- 1 litre (1 quart) water or beef stock (see recipe p. 24)
- salt and freshly ground black pepper

Right:
Stracciatella

- 4-8 eggs
- 4-8 slices home-style bread, toasted
- 4 tablespoons freshly grated aged pecorino cheese, preferably Tuscan

Wine: a dry white

(Galestro)

minutes the eggs will have set but will still be soft. § Arrange the slices of bread in individual soup bowls and ladle out the soup with one or two eggs per serving. Sprinkle with pecorino and serve.

VARIATIONS
— Beat the eggs and cheese together first. Pour them into the soup and stir rapidly with a fork or whisk for 1 minute before serving.
— Add a handful of cleaned and sliced fresh porcini or other wild mushrooms together with the tomatoes. Reduce the quantity of tomatoes by a quarter.
— Add a green pepper (capsicum) cut into thin strips.
— For a spicier soup, add ¼ teaspoon of crushed chillies and 1 clove of finely chopped garlic to the tomatoes.

Risi e bisi
Rice and pea soup

This famous Venetian soup is so thick that in the rest of Italy it would be called a risotto.

Serves 4; Preparation: 10 minutes; Cooking: 30 minutes; Level of difficulty: Simple

Melt half the butter in a pot together with the oil. Add the onion and sauté over low heat until soft and translucent. § Add the parsley and garlic and sauté for another 2-3 minutes. § Add the peas and a few tablespoons of stock, cover and cook over low heat for 8-10 minutes. § Stir in the remaining stock and the rice and cook for 13-14 minutes. § Taste to see if the rice is cooked. Season with salt and pepper. § Add the remaining butter and finish cooking. This will probably take another 2-3 minutes, depending on the rice. § Add the parmesan, mix well, and serve immediately.

VARIATIONS
– Add about 60 g (2 oz) of diced lean pancetta or coarsely chopped prosciutto when sautéing.
– For a fresher flavour, add the parsley just before serving the soup.

Minestra di fave
Broad bean soup

This dish is a speciality of Puglia, on the southern "heel" of Italy.

Serves 4; Preparation: 5 minutes + 10 hours to soak the beans; Cooking: 3 hours; Level of difficulty: Simple

Soak the broad beans in enough cold water to cover them amply for 8-10 hours. § Drain and transfer to a heavy-bottomed pan or earthenware pot. Add enough salted water to cover them by about 5 cm (2 in) above the level of the beans. § Cook over low heat for 3 hours, stirring frequently and mashing the broad beans with a fork. They should be completely disintegrated when cooked. § Add the oil, salt and pepper and serve immediately.

VARIATIONS
– In some areas of Puglia this dense cream is served with wild chicory, boiled in salted water and well drained.
– Thinly slice 1 red onion and soak in cold water for 30 minutes, changing the water a couple of times. Drain and season with oil, vinegar, salt and pepper. Add the onion to the soup just before serving.

■ INGREDIENTS
- 3 tablespoons butter
- 3 tablespoons extra-virgin olive oil
- 1 small onion, finely chopped
- ½ clove garlic
- 1 tablespoon finely chopped parsley
- 350 g (11 oz) shelled baby peas
- 1 litre (1 quart) boiling beef stock (see recipe p. 24)
- 250 g (8 oz) rice
- salt and freshly ground white pepper
- 4 tablespoons freshly grated parmesan cheese

Wine: a dry white (Soave)

■ INGREDIENTS
- 450 g (14 oz) dried broad beans
- 5-6 tablespoons of extra-virgin olive oil
- salt and freshly ground black pepper

Wine: a dry red (Cacc'à Mmitte di Lucera)

Right: *Risi e bisi*

MACCO DI FAVE
Crushed broad beans

The origins of this dish go back to Ancient Roman times when mushes based on legumes or grains were an important part of the diet. The name comes from maccare *or "to crush". It is common, with variations, throughout southern Italy. This recipe comes from Calabria.*

Serves 4; Preparation: 15 minutes + 10 hours to soak the beans; Cooking: 3 hours; Level of difficulty: Simple

Soak the broad beans in enough cold water to cover for 8-10 hours. § Combine 2 tablespoons of oil, the drained broad beans, the tomato, onion and celery in a heavy-bottomed pan or earthenware pot. Add 1.5 litres (1½ quarts) of water. § Partially cover and cook over low heat for 3 hours, stirring frequently and mashing the broad beans with a fork. They should be a soft purée. § When cooked, add salt, pepper and the remaining oil. § Serve the grated pecorino passed separately at table.

■ INGREDIENTS

- 250 g (8 oz) dried broad beans
- 200 g (6½ oz) peeled and chopped fresh or tinned tomatoes
- 5 tablespoons extra-virgin olive oil
- 1 large red onion, thinly sliced or chopped
- 3 celery stalks, cleaned and chopped
- salt and freshly ground black pepper
- 3 tablespoons freshly grated aged pecorino cheese (optional)

*Wine: a dry red
(San Severo Rosso)*

VARIATION
– In the Sicilian version of this dish, the celery is replaced with a small bunch of wild fennel (green part only).

CANEDERLI
Bread dumplings

The name derives from the German Knödel, *a preparation to be found, with variations, in many areas of central Europe. This version is from Trentino-Alto Adige in northeastern Italy. These large dumplings can be served in a soup as described here, or as a side dish with braised meat.*

Serves 4; Preparation: 45 minutes; Cooking: 15 minutes; Level of difficulty: Medium

Combine half the milk with the bread in a large bowl and let stand for at least 30 minutes, mixing once or twice. The bread should become soft but not too wet. If necessary, add the remaining milk. § Squeeze out the excess milk by hand and put the bread back in the bowl, discarding the milk first. § Gradually add the eggs, sausage,

■ INGREDIENTS

- about 250 ml (1 cup) milk
- 250 g (8 oz) densely-textured day-old bread, cut in pieces
- 2 eggs
- 90 g (3 oz) fresh Italian pork sausage, skinned and crumbled
- 90 g (3 oz) finely chopped smoked pancetta
- 90 g (3 oz) finely chopped prosciutto

Right: Canederli

- 1 tablespoon onion, finely chopped
- 2 tablespoons finely chopped parsley
- 75 g (2½ oz) white flour
- salt
- 1 litre (1 quart) boiling beef stock (see recipe p. 24)

White: a dry white (Terlano)

pancetta, prosciutto, onion, half the parsley and 3 scant tablespoons of flour, stirring continuously until the mixture is firm but elastic. If needed, add a little more flour. § In the meantime, bring 750 ml (3 cups) of water to a boil with 2 tablespoons salt in a fairly deep pot. § Make small balls about 5 cm (2 in) in diameter with the bread mixture and dust with flour. § When they are all ready, drop the *canederli* into the pot of boiling water. Turn the heat up to high until the water begins to boil, then lower the heat slightly and cook for 15 minutes. § Remove from the water with a skimmer. Drain, transfer to a tureen, and ladle in the boiling stock. Garnish with the parsley.

FRITTATINE IN BRODO
Crêpes in stock

Despite the French name, crêpes are actually an Italian invention. According to tradition, they were first made in the 5th century. Later they became very popular in France and from there spread throughout the world. This recipe is a specialty of Abruzzo, in southern Italy.

Serves 4; Preparation: 10 minutes; Cooking: 30 minutes; Level of difficulty: Medium

Beat the eggs in a bowl with 1 heaped tablespoon of pecorino, the parsley, salt, nutmeg, and one-third of the milk. § Gradually add the flour, alternating with the remaining milk. The batter should be fairly liquid. § Melt a quarter of the lard in a small, nonstick frying pan, about 15-18 cm (6-7 in) in diameter. When it is sizzling hot, pour in two spoonfuls of batter. § Tip the frying pan and rotate, so that the batter spreads out to form a very thin crêpe. After less than a minute, turn it over with a spatula and cook for another minute or less on the other side. § Slide it onto a plate and repeat, adding a dab of shortening to the frying pan each time, until all the batter has been used. Stack the crêpes up in a pile. These quantities should make about 12 crêpes. § Dust each one with ½ tablespoon of pecorino. Roll them up loosely and arrange in individual soup bowls, three per person. § Pour the boiling stock over the top and serve with the remaining cheese.

■ INGREDIENTS

- 3 eggs
- 150 g (5 oz) grated pecorino cheese
- ½ tablespoon finely chopped parsley
- salt
- pinch of nutmeg
- 125 ml (½ cup) milk
- 6-7 tablespoons white flour
- 1 heaped tablespoon lard
- 1 litre (1 quart) boiling chicken stock (see recipe p. 24)

Wine: a dry white (Trebbiano d'Abruzzo)

PAPPA CON IL POMODORO
Bread soup with tomato

This Tuscan soup is a delicious way of using up leftover bread.

Serves 4; Preparation: 15 minutes; Cooking: 20-25 minutes: Level of difficulty: Simple

Put the diced bread in a preheated oven at 160°C/325°F for 10 minutes to dry it out, but without toasting. § In the meantime, plunge the tomatoes into boiling water for 10 seconds and then into cold. Peel and cut them in half horizontally. Squeeze gently to remove most of the seeds and chop the flesh into small pieces. § Pour 6 tablespoons of the oil into a heavy-bottomed pan or earthenware pot and add the garlic and bay leaves. § As

■ INGREDIENTS

- 250 g (8 oz) densely textured bread, sliced and cubed
- 8 tablespoons extra-virgin olive oil
- 3 cloves garlic, crushed
- 1-2 bay leaves
- salt and freshly ground black pepper

Right:
Pappa con il pomodoro

- 400 g (14 oz) firm ripe tomatoes
- about 250 ml (1 cup) water

Wine: a dry white
(Bianco Vergine Val di Chiana)

soon as the oil is hot, add the diced bread and cook over medium-low heat for 3-4 minutes, stirring frequently. § Season with salt and pepper. § Stir in the tomatoes and, using a ladle, add just under 500 ml (2 cups) of water. § Cook for 15 minutes, stirring occasionally. If the soup becomes too thick, add a little more water (remember, however, that it should be very thick). § Drizzle the remaining oil over the top and serve hot.

VARIATIONS
— Replace the bay leaves with a dozen fresh basil leaves and add them with the tomatoes.
— If you prefer a more liquid soup, cut the bread in thin slices, dip quickly in water, without toasting at all, and continue as above, stirring frequently during the cooking process so that the result will be a sort of porridge.

Dadolini in Brodo
Dice in beef or chicken stock

This recipe comes from Friuli but similar dishes are to be found in other regions as well. The dice are suited to most light, cream of vegetable soups.

Serves 4; Preparation: 10 minutes; Cooking: 1 hour; Level of difficulty: Simple

Combine the eggs, lukewarm melted butter, parmesan, salt and nutmeg to taste in a bowl. Mix well with a fork, then slowly add the flour to the mixture, making sure that no lumps form. § Pour the mixture into a lightly buttered square or rectangular nonstick pan, large enough so that when the mixture is smoothly spread out in the pan, it will be no more than 2 cm (¾-in) deep. § Bake in a preheated oven at 150°C/300°F for 1 hour. § Cut into squares when cool. Add to the tureen and pour the stock in over the top. § Serve immediately.

■ INGREDIENTS

• 3 large eggs
• 3 tablespoons melted butter
• 90 g (3 oz) freshly grated parmesan cheese
• 90 g (3 oz) white flour
• salt
• pinch of nutmeg
• 1.2 litres (5 cups) boiling beef or chicken stock (see recipes p. 24)

Wine: a dry white (Verduzzo "Grave del Friuli")

Zuppa Mariconda
Dumplings in beef or chicken stock

This delicate soup from Brescia and Mantua in the north, first appears in cookbooks dating from the 16th century, but the origin of the name remains a mystery.

Serves 4; Preparation: 40 minutes + 1 hour in the refrigerator; Cooking: 5-7 minutes; Level of difficulty: Simple

Put the bread in a bowl and soften it with the milk, stirring a couple of times. After 15-20 minutes, drain and squeeze out some, but not all, of the milk. § In a nonstick saucepan, melt the butter, add the bread, and let it dry out over low heat, mixing well. This will take a couple of minutes. The bread will still be soft because it will have absorbed the butter. § Transfer to a bowl and add the eggs, parmesan, nutmeg and salt and pepper to taste. Mix well to obtain a smooth mixture. § Cover with plastic wrap or a plate and place in the refrigerator for about 1 hour. § Take teaspoonfuls of the mixture to make small dumplings, about the size of a large marble, and line them up on a cutting board, large plate, or a sheet of aluminum foil. § Bring the stock to a boil in a fairly deep pot, and drop in the dumplings. § Lower the heat as soon as the stock begins to boil again. When the dumplings are cooked they will rise to the surface. § Serve immediately, with extra grated parmesan, if desired.

■ INGREDIENTS

• 200 g (6½ oz) day-old bread, without the crust, broken into pieces
• about 250 ml (1 cup) milk
• 4 tablespoons butter
• 3 eggs
• 5 tablespoons freshly grated parmesan cheese
• pinch of nutmeg
• salt and freshly grated white pepper (optional)
• 1.2 litres (5 cups) beef or chicken stock (see recipes p. 24)

Wine: a light, dry white (Collio Goriziano)

Right:
Dadolini in brodo

INGREDIENTS

- 300 g (10 oz) dried chick peas
- 200 g (6½ oz) young Swiss chard (silver beet), cleaned and washed
- 3-4 tablespoons extra-virgin olive oil
- 1 medium onion, finely chopped
- 1-2 cloves garlic, whole but lightly crushed
- 3-4 anchovy fillets in oil
- 3 plum tomatoes, peeled and chopped, or 1 tablespoon tomato paste
- 2 litres (2 quarts) boiling water
- salt and freshly ground black pepper
- 4-8 slices dense grain, home-style bread, toasted
- 4 tablespoons freshly grated aged pecorino cheese, preferably Tuscan

Wine: a dry white (Montecarlo)

Caciucco di ceci
Chick pea soup

Soups using chick peas are common throughout Italy. This recipe comes from the area around Pisa, in Tuscany.

Serves 4; Preparation: 30 minutes + the time needed to soak the chick peas; Cooking: 3½ hours; Level of difficulty: Medium

Place the chick peas in a bowl and add enough cold water to cover them by at least 5 cm (2 in). Soak for 12 hours (It might take as long as 24 hours if the chick peas are a year or more old). § About 3½ hours before you intend to serve the soup, put the Swiss chard, well rinsed but not drained dry, in a pot and cook, covered, for about 5 minutes over medium heat. Set aside. § Heat the oil over medium heat in a large heavy-bottomed pan or earthenware pot. Add the onion and garlic and sauté until the onion is soft and translucent. § Add the anchovy fillets, mashing them with a fork as you stir. § Drain the chick peas and add to the pot, together with the chard and the liquid it was cooked in, and the tomatoes (or tomato paste). Season with salt and pepper, stir, and add about 2 litres (2 quarts) of hot water. § Cover the pot and simmer over medium heat for at least 3 hours. The chick peas should be very tender. § Taste for salt and pepper. § Arrange the slices of bread in individual soup bowls and ladle the soup over the top. § Sprinkle with the pecorino and serve.

VARIATION
– Use 500 g (1 lb) of drained, canned chick peas. This will cut out the lengthy soaking process. In this case reduce the cooking time to just over 30 minutes. Only about about 1 litre (1 quart) of water will be required.

Left:
Cacciucco di ceci

Minestra di riso e patate
Rice and potato soup

Serves 4; Preparation: 20 minutes; Cooking: 20-25 minutes; Level of difficulty: Simple

Put the pancetta, onion and rosemary in a pot and sauté over low heat for 2-3 minutes, stirring frequently. § Add the potatoes and the stock. As soon as it begins to boil, add the rice, stir once or twice and cook for 15 minutes. § Taste for salt and to see if the rice is cooked. Add the parsley just before serving, and pass the cheese separately.

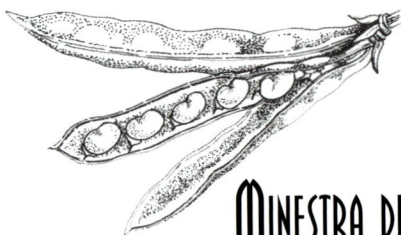

Minestra di riso e fagioli
Rice and bean soup

Cannellini or white beans are not available fresh throughout the year, and soaking and cooking dried beans requires time and forethought. This recipe for a typically Tuscan soup is based on tinned beans.

Serves 4; Preparation: 25 minutes; Cooking: 40-45 minutes; Level of difficulty: Medium

Put the oil, pancetta, onion, celery, garlic, parsley, basil, chillies and sage in a pot, preferably earthenware. Cook over low heat for 7-8 minutes, stirring occasionally. § In the meantime plunge the tomatoes into boiling water for 10 seconds, then into cold. Peel them and cut in half horizontally. Squeeze lightly to remove most of the seeds. Chop the flesh coarsely and stir them into the pot. § Simmer for 15 minutes, covered, stirring occasionally. § Add the beans and the 1 litre (1 quart) of boiling stock (or water) and cook for another 5 minutes. § Add the rice which will take about 15 minutes to cook. If necessary, add a little more boiling stock or water (although bear in mind that the soup should be quite thick). Season with salt and serve hot.

VARIATIONS
— Use 450 g (14 oz) canned tomatoes, well drained and chopped, in place of the fresh tomatoes.
— This soup can be served lukewarm or cold (at room temperature) particularly in summer. In that case cook the rice for just 10 minutes.

Right: Minestra di riso e patate

ZUPPA DI CIPOLLE
Onion soup

Serves 4; Preparation: 15 minutes; Cooking: 40 minutes; Level of difficulty: Simple

Combine the onions, oil, celery and carrot in a deep, heavy-bottomed saucepan or earthenware pot. Cover and sauté over low heat, stirring frequently. § After 20 minutes season with salt and pepper. § Continue cooking, stirring and adding a spoonful or so of the stock, for another 20 minutes. § Dilute with the remaining stock. § Place the toast in a tureen or individual soup bowls and pour the soup over the top. Sprinkle with the pecorino and serve.

ZUPPA DI VALPELLINE
Valpelline soup

This delicious soup comes from a village called Valpelline in the Valle d'Aosta in the northwest.

Serves 4; Preparation: 20 minutes; Cooking: 1 hour; Level of difficulty: Medium

Clean the cabbage and cut in quarters, discarding the core so that the leaves are no longer attached. § Melt the lard in a saucepan over low heat, add the cabbage leaves, cover and cook for 10-15 minutes, stirring occasionally. § Dry the bread out in a preheated oven at 150°C/300°F for 15 minutes. Make sure it doesn't get too dark. § Arrange a layer of toasted slices on the bottom of a large ovenproof baking dish and drizzle with 2 tablespoons of pan juices. Cover with one-third of the prosciutto and one-third of the cabbage. Season with a sprinkling of the spices and distribute one-third of the fontina on top. Repeat the procedure twice. § Before adding the last layer of fontina, pour on as much stock as needed to just cover the layers. § Arrange the remaining fontina on the top and dot with dabs of butter. § Place the dish in a preheated oven at 150°C/300°F and gradually increase the temperature (in 15 minutes it should reach 200°C/400°F). Cook for 30-40 minutes. § Serve hot straight from the oven.

■ INGREDIENTS

- 1 kg (2 lb) red onions, cut in thin slices
- 7 tablespoons extra-virgin olive oil
- 1 small celery stalk, finely chopped
- 1 small carrot, finely chopped (optional)
- salt and freshly ground pepper
- 1 litre (1 quart) boiling beef stock (see recipe p. 24)
- 4 slices toasted bread
- 4 tablespoons freshly grated aged pecorino cheese

Wine: a dry white
(Bianco dei Colli Maceratesi)

■ INGREDIENTS

- 1 medium Savoy cabbage
- 30 g (1 oz) lard
- 8-10 slices toasted bread
- 125 ml (½ cup) pan juices from a roast
- 150 g (5 oz) prosciutto, finely chopped
- pinch of nutmeg
- pinch of ground cloves
- pinch of ground cinnamon
- 200 g (6½ oz) fontina cheese, cut in thin slivers
- 1 litre (1 quart) meat stock (see recipe p. 24)
- 2 tablespoons butter

Wine: a dry, fruity white
(Blanc de Morgex)

Right:
Zuppa di cipolle

INGREDIENTS

- 1 kg (2 lb) turnips, cleaned and sliced
- 150 g (5 oz) diced lean pancetta
- 60 g (2 oz) finely chopped lard
- 1 clove garlic, finely chopped
- 1.5 litres (1½ quarts) boiling beef stock (see recipe p. 24)
- 4-8 slices toasted bread
- salt and freshly ground black pepper
- 5 tablespoons freshly grated parmesan cheese

Wine: a dry white
(Bianco di Custoza)

INGREDIENTS

- 30 g (1 oz) dried porcini mushrooms
- ½ tablespoon finely chopped calamint or parsley
- 1 clove garlic, finely chopped
- 5 tablespoons extra-virgin olive oil
- 650 g (1¼ lb) porcini (or white) mushrooms, sliced
- 125 ml (½ cup) dry white wine
- 1 litre (1 quart) boiling vegetable stock (see recipe p. 22)
- 1 tablespoon white flour
- salt and freshly ground pepper
- 4 slices toasted bread

Wine: a light, dry rosé
(Colli Altotiberini Rosato)

Left:
Zuppa di funghi

ZUPPA DI RAPE
Turnip soup

A rustic, winter soup from Piedmont in the north.

Serves 4; Preparation: 20 minutes; Cooking: 30 minutes: Level of difficulty: Simple

Put the turnips, pancetta, lard and garlic in a heavy-bottomed saucepan. Add the stock, cover, and simmer over low heat for 30 minutes. § Season with salt and pepper. § Arrange the toast in individual soup bowls, sprinkle with half the cheese, and pour the soup over the top. § Serve the rest of the cheese passed separately.

VARIATIONS
— Sauté the pancetta, lard, and garlic for 4-5 minutes. Add the turnips, stir and sauté 2 more minutes before adding the stock.
— Serve the soup in a tureen, alternating a layer of toast sprinkled with cheese with 2 ladles of soup.

ZUPPA DI FUNGHI
Mushroom soup

If you can't get fresh porcini, use the same quantity of white mushrooms.
In this case, double the quantity of dried porcini.

Serves 4; Preparation: 40 minutes; Cooking: 35-40 minutes; Level of difficulty: Medium

Soak the dried porcini mushrooms in 250 ml (1 cup) of tepid water for 30 minutes, then drain and chop finely. § Strain the water in which they were soaked and set aside. § Sauté the calamint (or parsley) and garlic with 4 tablespoons of oil in a heavy-bottomed saucepan over medium heat for 30 seconds. § Add the dried mushrooms, and after a couple of minutes, the fresh mushrooms. Sauté for about 5 minutes, stirring occasionally. § Pour in the wine, and after a couple of minutes, begin gradually adding the stock and mushroom water. § Simmer for about 25 minutes. § Heat the remaining oil in a frying pan over low heat. Add the flour and brown slightly, stirring carefully. § Remove the frying pan from the heat and add 3-4 tablespoons of the mushroom liquid, mixing well so that no lumps form. § Pour this mixture into the soup. Cook another 2-3 minutes, stirring continuously. § Arrange the bread in individual soup bowls, or in a tureen, and pour the soup over the top.

ZUPPA DI ACCIUGHE

Fresh anchovy soup

Serves 4; Preparation: 30 minutes; Cooking: 25 minutes; Level of difficulty: Medium

Combine the oil, onion, celery, carrot, parsley, garlic and chillies in a heavy-bottomed saucepan or earthenware pot and sauté over low heat for 6-7 minutes or until the mixture becomes soft. § Plunge the tomatoes into a pot of boiling water for 10 seconds and then into cold. Drain and peel. § Cut them in half horizontally, and squeeze to remove some of the seeds. Chop coarsely. § Add to the pan and continue cooking for about 10 minutes. § Add the anchovies, pour in the wine, and stir carefully. § Simmer for 5-8 minutes over low heat adding about 500 ml (2 cups) of salted boiling water a little at a time. Don't stir during this stage, just shake the pan occasionally. § Pour the soup into individual soup bowls over the slices of toasted bread and serve.

■ INGREDIENTS

- 4 tablespoons extra-virgin olive oil
- ½ small onion, ½ celery stalk, ½ small carrot, all finely chopped
- ½ tablespoon finely chopped parsley
- 1 clove garlic, finely chopped
- ¼ teaspoon crushed chillies
- 2 medium-large tomatoes
- 1 kg (2 lb) anchovies, without their heads, cleaned and boned
- 250 ml (1 cup) white wine
- salt
- 4-8 slices toasted bread

*Wine: a dry white
(Pigato di Albenga)*

ZUPPA DI MOSCARDINI

Octopus soup

Moscardini are a kind of tiny octopus. If you can't get them fresh or frozen, use very small squid in their place. To clean them, turn the head inside out like a glove, remove the inner organs, and discard the eyes and the beak (the white ball in the middle of the base of the tentacles).

Serves 4; Preparation: 20 minutes; Cooking: 40 minutes; Level of difficulty: Simple

Plunge the tomatoes into boiling water for 10 seconds, then into cold, slip off the skins, and cut into pieces. § Heat the oil with the parsley and garlic in a heavy-bottomed saucepan or an earthenware pot. § Add the *moscardini* and braise for 3 minutes over medium heat, stirring continuously. § Add the wine and when this has evaporated, add the tomatoes, chillies and a little salt. § Stir one last time and cover the pot— the moscardini produce a good deal of liquid which, together with that of the tomatoes, has to be kept from evaporating. Cook for 30 minutes, shaking the pot frequently. § Finally, taste for salt and pour the soup over slices of toasted bread in a tureen or individual bowls.

■ INGREDIENTS

- 4 medium tomatoes, ripe and firm
- 4 tablespoons extra-virgin olive oil
- 1 tablespoon finely chopped parsley
- 1 clove garlic, finely chopped
- 750 g (1½ lb) moscardini, cleaned, rinsed, and cut in pieces
- 125 ml (½ cup) dry white wine
- ¼ teaspoon crushed chillies
- salt
- 4-8 slices toasted bread

*Wine: a dry white
(Vernaccia di San Gimignano)*

Right:
Zuppa di moscardini

VARIATIONS
– Add 1 teaspoon of fresh finely chopped rosemary with the tomatoes.
– For extra fragrance, add 2 tablespoons of olive oil just before serving.

Rice and Risotti

Rice is such a versatile food and the possibilities for serving it Italian-style are almost endless. Remember that only short-grain rice is grown in Italy; most long-grain varieties are not suitable for these recipes.

Insalata di riso arcobaleno
Rainbow rice salad

The mixture of salty and sweet ingredients in this salad is refreshing. Like all rice salads, the rice can be cooked in advance.

Serves 4; Preparation: 30 minutes; Cooking: 15 minutes; Level of difficulty: Simple

Bring 2 litres (2 quarts) of salted water to a boil. Add the rice, stir once or twice, and allow 13-15 minutes cooking time from when the water comes to a boil again. The rice should be *al dente* but not too firm. § Drain, pass under cold running water for 30 seconds to stop cooking. Drain again very thoroughly and transfer to a large salad bowl. § Season with oil, lemon juice and pepper to taste. § Just before serving, add the remaining ingredients and toss well.

Insalata di riso semplicissima
Simple rice salad

Rice is a very versatile ingredient in any salad. This is a basic Italian rice salad. The possible variations are almost infinite (I have suggested a few of the more popular ones at the end of the recipe). Use your imagination to create your own variations.

Serves 4; Preparation: 30 minutes; Cooking: 15 minutes; Level of difficulty: Simple

Bring 2 litres (2 quarts) of salted water to a boil. Add the rice, stir once or twice, and allow 13-15 minutes cooking time from when the water comes to a boil again. The rice should be *al dente* but not too firm.

■ INGREDIENTS

- 250 g (8 oz) rice
- 4 tablespoons extra-virgin olive oil
- 2 tablespoons lemon juice
- salt and freshly ground white pepper
- 2 medium tomatoes, cubed
- 6-8 red radishes, trimmed and sliced
- 2 small celery stalks, sliced
- 6 pickled gherkins, sliced
- 8 small white pickled onions, quartered
- 1 tablespoon well-washed salted capers
- 10 large sweet green olives in brine, pitted and quartered
- 1 heaped tablespoon sultana raisins, rinsed and drained
- 2 tablespoons blanched almonds
- 125 g (4 oz) parmesan cheese, flaked

Wine: a dry white (Bianco di Custoza)

■ INGREDIENTS

- 250 g (8 oz) rice
- 4 tablespoons extra-virgin olive oil
- 2 medium firm tomatoes
- 1 medium cucumber, peeled and cubed
- 1 tablespoon capers
- 10 green or black olives, pitted and chopped

Right:
Insalata di riso semplicissima

- 125 g (4 oz) Emmental
  cheese, cubed
- 6 leaves fresh basil, torn

Wine: a dry white
(Sauvignon Isonzo)

§ Drain, pass under cold running water for 30 seconds to stop cooking. Drain again very thoroughly and transfer to a large salad bowl. § Toss with the oil immediately. § Just before serving add the remaining ingredients and mix well.

VARIATIONS
— Garnish the salad with 150 g (5 oz) mayonnaise mixed with ½ teaspoon French mustard.
— For a more substantial dish, add 125 g (4 oz) tuna fish in chunks, or 150 g (5 oz) boiled, julienne-cut chicken.
— Garnish with any of the following: thin slices of lemon, cut in half; anchovy fillets in oil, either cut in pieces or rolled; wedges of hard-boiled egg; quartered artichoke hearts or baby mushrooms in oil; ½ tablespoon of chopped chives.

INSALATA DI RISO CON GAMBERETTI
Rice salad with shrimp

INGREDIENTS

- 800 g (1¾ lb) raw shrimp in shell
- juice of 1 lemon, plus 3 tablespoons
- 6 tablespoons extra-virgin olive oil
- 450 g (14 oz) rice
- 4 tablespoons coarsely chopped arugula (rocket)
- salt and freshly ground white pepper

Wine: a dry white (Pinot Bianco di Latisana)

This salad makes an appetizing main course and can be prepared ahead of time.

Serves 4; Preparation: 30 minutes; Cooking: 15-20 minutes; Level of difficulty: Medium

Bring 2 litres (2 quarts) of salted water and the juice of 1 lemon to a boil. Add the shrimp and cook over high heat for 5 minutes. § Drain, let the shrimp cool slightly and shell: detach the head, press the tail with two fingers at its base, and the body will slip out. § Put the shrimp in a bowl with almost all the oil. § Cook the rice in 2.5 litres (2½ quarts) of salted, boiling water, stirring occasionally and allowing 13-15 minutes cooking time from when the water comes to a boil again. § When the rice is cooked, drain and pass under cold running water. Drain thoroughly and transfer to the bowl with the shrimp. § Mix carefully, and add pepper to taste. Check if more salt is needed and add the remaining lemon juice and oil. § Just before serving, add the arugula and mix again.

> VARIATION
> – Shelling shrimp is not complicated but it can be tedious. It may be easier to buy shelled boiled shrimp in brine which only have to be drained and rinsed: they are excellent. Alternatively, use frozen shelled shrimp which only have to be boiled for a few minutes.

RISO CON FEGATINI
Rice with chicken livers

INGREDIENTS

- 450 g (14 oz) rice
- 4 tablespoons butter
- 1 small onion, finely chopped
- 30 g (1 oz) pine nuts
- 8 chicken livers, chopped
- salt and freshly ground white pepper
- 5 tablespoons dry marsala
- 5 tablespoons dry white wine

Wine: a dry white (Müller Thurgau)

Left:
Insalata di riso con gamberetti

The sauce can be made ahead of time and heated up when ready to serve.

Serves 4; Preparation: 10 minutes; Cooking: 15 minutes; Level of difficulty: Simple

Pour the rice into 2 litres (2 quarts) of salted, boiling water and stir well. Allow 13-15 minutes cooking time from when the water comes to a boil again. § Melt the butter in a saucepan, add the onion, and sauté for 3 minutes. § Turn the heat up to medium-high, add the chicken livers (check to make sure that the bile sacks have been removed and chop off any green spots), pine nuts, salt and pepper. Stir for 1-2 minutes to brown and then add half the marsala and wine, stir again and add the rest. § Cook for 6-7 minutes, stirring occasionally. § When the rice is cooked, drain thoroughly and transfer to a serving dish. § Pour the chicken liver sauce over the top and serve hot.

RISO ALL'UOVO
Rice with egg and cream

■ INGREDIENTS

- 450 g (14 oz) rice
- 3 fresh egg yolks
- scant 100 ml (3½ fl oz) light cream
- 4 tablespoons freshly grated parmesan cheese
- freshly ground white pepper (optional)
- 1½ tablespoons butter

Wine: a dry white
(Traminer Aromatico)

Serves 4; Preparation: 2 minutes; Cooking: 13-15 minutes; Level of difficulty: Simple

Pour the rice in 2 litres (2 quarts) of boiling salted water, stirring once or twice. Allow 13-15 minutes cooking time from when the water comes to a boil again. § When the rice is almost done, mix the egg yolks, cream, parmesan and a pinch of pepper, if desired, in a bowl. § Drain the rice thoroughly, catching the cooking water in the serving bowl to heat it. Pour out the water, transfer the rice and season with the sauce and dabs of butter. Stir quickly and serve immediately.

RISO INTEGRALE CON SALSA DI POMODORO CRUDO
Brown rice with uncooked tomato sauce

■ INGREDIENTS

- riso integrale, 350-400 g
- pomodori ben maturi ma sodi, 500 g
- olio extra vergine d'oliva, 4-5 cucchiai
- 1 piccola cipolla, a fettine sottili
- aglio, intero o tritato, 1 spicchio
- origano o maggiorana, 1 pizzico generoso
- peperoncino rosso essiccato, sbriciolato, 1 pezzetto
- basilico fresco, spezzettato a mano, 5-7 foglie

Vino: rosato leggero
(Chiaretto del Garda)

The combination of brown rice and tomato sauce is always delicious. For winter meals, serve the brown rice with basic tomato sauce (see recipe p. 22). In summer, when fresh tomatoes are readily available and soaring temperatures make life in the kitchen unpleasant, serve this simple uncooked sauce on hot or cold brown rice.

Serves 4; Preparation: 25 minutes; Cooking: 45 minutes; Level of difficulty: Simple

Cook the rice in 2 litres (2 quarts) of salted, boiling water, stirring once or twice. It will be cooked in about 45 minutes. § Wash the tomatoes and chop them in half. Leave upside-down in a colander to drain for about 20 minutes. § Chop the tomatoes coarsely and transfer to a bowl. § Add 3 tablespoons of the oil, the onion, garlic, oregano or marjoram, basil, salt and pepper. Mix carefully. § When the rice is done, drain thoroughly, and transfer to a large bowl (a wooden bowl is very attractive with the brown tones of the rice). § Pour the remaining oil over the rice and toss vigorously. § Add the tomato and herb mixture, toss carefully and serve.

VARIATIONS
— Add 90 g (3 oz) diced mozzarella cheese and a handful of large black olives to the salad before serving.
— Crumble 2 anchovy fillets into the tomato sauce with the herbs.
— Add 1 tablespoon of small salted capers to the tomato sauce.

Right: Riso integrale
con salsa di pomodoro crudo

RISOTTO CON ASPARAGI
Asparagus risotto

The delicate flavours in this risotto call for high-quality, fresh asparagus.

Serves 4; Preparation: 15 minutes; Cooking: 25 minutes; Level of difficulty: Medium

Rinse the asparagus and trim the stalks to 12 mm (½ in) before the white part begins. Cut the green tips in two or three pieces. § Melt 3 tablespoons of butter in a deep, heavy-bottomed saucepan. Add the onion and sauté for 1 minute; then add the asparagus and sauté for 5 minutes. § Add the rice and pour in the wine. Stir well. § When the wine has all been absorbed, begin adding the boiling stock, a little at a time, stirring frequently. § The risotto will be cooked in 15-18 minutes. § Add the remaining butter and the parmesan. Mix well. § Check the seasoning and add salt and pepper if required.

■ INGREDIENTS

- 800 g (1¾ lb) asparagus
- 4 tablespoons butter
- 1 small onion, finely chopped
- 350 g (11 oz) arborio rice
- 125 ml (½ cup) dry white wine
- 1 litre (1 quart) beef stock (see recipe p. 24)
- 4 tablespoons freshly grated parmesan cheese
- salt and freshly ground white pepper

Wine: a dry white (Erbaluce di Caluso)

RISOTTO ALLA SBIRRAGLIA
Chicken risotto

Served with a green salad, this nourishing risotto is a meal in itself. It takes its name from the Austrian soldiers (sbirri) who occupied northern Italy in the 19th century. They were apparently very fond of it.

Serves 4; Preparation: 10 minutes: Cooking: 1 hour; Level of difficulty: Medium

Melt 2 tablespoons butter together with the oil in a deep, heavy-bottomed saucepan. Add the celery, onion and carrot and sauté for 2 minutes over low heat. § Season the chicken with salt and pepper and place the pieces in the saucepan in a single layer. Increase the heat and brown, turning the chicken as required. § After 8-10 minutes begin sprinkling with wine. Cover and continue cooking, gradually adding the wine, for 25-30 minutes. § To test if the chicken is cooked, pierce with a fork or toothpick. The liquid that forms around the hole should be transparent rather than pink. § Remove the chicken and set aside in a warm oven or on a dish set over a pot of very hot water and covered with another dish. § Place the rice and chicken livers in the pan with the cooking juices and cook for 1 minute. § Gradually stir in the boiling stock. Continue cooking until the rice is tender, stirring frequently (it will take about 15-18 minutes). § Just before serving, add the remaining butter and parmesan and mix well. § Transfer the risotto to a serving dish and arrange the pieces of chicken on top.

■ INGREDIENTS

- 3 tablespoons butter
- 3 tablespoons extra-virgin olive oil
- 1 small celery stalk, 1 small onion, 1 small carrot, finely chopped
- 1 chicken, ready to cook, weighing about 1 kg (2 lb), cut in 8 pieces
- salt and freshly ground white pepper
- 250 ml (1 cup) dry white wine
- 350 g (11 oz) arborio rice
- 1.2 litres (5 cups) boiling beef stock (see recipe p. 24)
- 1 chicken liver, cleaned and finely chopped
- 2 tablespoons freshly grated parmesan cheese

Wine: a dry red (Galestro)

Right: Risotto con asparagi

INGREDIENTS

- 5 tablespoons extra-virgin olive oil
- ½ onion, finely chopped
- 350 g (11 oz) arborio rice
- 5 bay leaves
- 500 ml (2 cups) dry white wine
- 750 ml (3 cups) boiling beef stock (see recipe p. 24)
- pinch of nutmeg
- salt

Wine: a dry white (Orvieto Bianco)

Risotto con alloro
Risotto with bay leaves

To savour the full flavour of this fragrant risotto, serve without adding parmesan cheese.

Serves 4; Preparation: 5 minutes; Cooking: 20 minutes; Level of difficulty: Simple

Heat the oil in a large heavy-bottomed saucepan and sauté the onion until it is soft and translucent. § Add the rice and bay leaves. Stir for 2 minutes and then begin adding the wine, a little at a time. § When all the wine has been absorbed, add the nutmeg and continue cooking. § Gradually stir in the stock until the rice is cooked. It will take about 15-18 minutes. § Serve hot.

RISOTTO AL PREZZEMOLO E BASILICO
Basil risotto

This traditional recipe contains all the fragrance of the Italian Riviera.

Serves 4; Preparation: 10 minutes; Cooking: 25 minutes; Level of difficulty: Simple

Dissolve the marrow in a heavy-bottomed saucepan over low heat. § Add the butter, oil and garlic, and sauté for 1 minute. § Add the rice and cook for 2 minutes, stirring constantly. § Begin adding the stock, a little at a time, stirring frequently. § The rice will take about 15-18 minutes to cook. § Add the basil and parsley a few minutes before the rice is ready. § Taste for salt and pepper. § Add the pecorino as the final touch and serve hot.

RISO ARROSTO
Roasted rice

The original recipe for this Ligurian speciality calls for the juices produced by a roast. Nowadays butter or oil are generally used instead.

Serves 4; Preparation: 35 minutes; Cooking: 45-50 minutes; Level of difficulty: Medium

In a large, heavy-bottomed saucepan melt three parts of the butter or oil. § Add the onion, sausage, mushrooms, artichokes and peas. Season with salt and pepper. § Stirring continuously, sauté over low heat for 5 minutes. § Add the stock, cover, and continue cooking for about 10 minutes. § In the meantime, bring 1.5 litres (1½ quarts) of salted water to a boil, pour in the rice and cook for 7-8 minutes. § Drain partially (leave some moisture). Transfer to the saucepan with the sauce and stir. Add the cheese and mix well. Transfer to an ovenproof dish greased with the remaining butter or oil. § Bake in a preheated oven at 200-220°C/400-425°F for about 20 minutes. The rice will have a light golden crust when ready.

VARIATION
– If fresh porcini mushrooms are unavailable, use 30 g (1 oz) dried porcini. Soak for at least 30 minutes in 250 ml (8fl oz) of tepid water, then drain, chop coarsely, and combine with 125 g (4 oz) sliced white mushrooms.

■ INGREDIENTS

- 2 tablespoons finely chopped ox-bone marrow
- 2 tablespoons butter
- 3 tablespoons extra-virgin olive oil
- 2 cloves garlic, finely chopped
- 350 g (11 oz) arborio rice
- 1.5 litres (1½ quarts) vegetable stock (see recipe p. 22)
- 1 tablespoon basil, 1 tablespoon parsley, finely chopped
- salt and white pepper
- 3 tablespoons freshly grated pecorino cheese

Wine: a dry white (Trebbiano)

■ INGREDIENTS

- 2½ tablespoons butter, or 4 tablespoons extra-virgin olive oil
- 1 small onion, finely chopped
- 150 g (5 oz) Italian pork sausage, skinned and crumbled
- 200 g (6½ oz) sliced fresh porcini mushrooms
- 2 globe artichokes, cleaned and thinly sliced
- 2 tablespoons peas
- salt and pepper
- 250 ml (1 cup) beef stock (see recipe p. 24)
- 350 g (11 oz) rice
- 3 tablespoons freshly grated pecorino cheese

Wine: a dry white (Vermentino)

Right:
Risotto al prezzemolo e basilico

RISOTTO AI CARCIOFI
Artichoke risotto

It is extremely important to clean the artichokes properly, discarding the tough tips, outer leaves and fuzzy choke. The inner hearts should be cut into slices less than 3 mm (⅛-in) thick.

Serves 4; Preparation: 20 minutes; Cooking: 30 minutes; Level of difficulty: Medium

Clean the artichokes as described and place in a bowl of cold water with the lemon juice. Soak for 10-15 minutes so they will not discolour. § Melt the butter in a large, heavy-bottomed saucepan. Add the onion and sauté for a few minutes. § Drain the artichoke slices and add to the onion; sauté for another 5 minutes. § Add the rice and stir for 2 minutes. Increase the heat slightly, and begin adding the boiling stock, a little at a time, until the rice is cooked. It will take about 15-18 minutes. Season with salt and pepper. § Add the parsley and pecorino at the last minute. Mix well to create a creamy risotto.

VARIATION
– For a slightly different flavour, replace half the butter with 3 tablespoons of extra-virgin olive oil.

■ INGREDIENTS

- 6-7 globe artichokes, cleaned and sliced
- juice of 1 lemon
- 3 tablespoons butter
- ½ small onion, finely chopped
- 350 g (11 fl oz) arborio rice
- 1.2 litres (5 cups) boiling water or vegetable stock (see recipe p. 22)
- salt and freshly ground black pepper
- 1 tablespoon finely chopped parsley
- 3 tablespoons freshly grated parmesan or pecorino romano cheese

Wine: a dry white (Vernaccia di San Giminiano)

RISO ALLA BIELLESE
Rice with butter and cheese

This dish comes from Piedmont and Valle d'Aosta in northwestern Italy where it was traditionally served at wedding banquets.

Serves 4; Preparation: 5 minutes; Cooking: 13-15 minutes; Level of difficulty: Simple

Pour the rice into 2 litres (2 quarts) of salted, boiling water and stir once or twice. Allow 13-15 minutes cooking time from when the water comes to a boil again. § A couple of minutes before the rice is cooked, melt the butter in a saucepan until it turns golden brown. § Drain the rice over the serving bowl so it fills with the hot cooking water. Don't drain the rice too thoroughly. § Throw out the water in the bowl which is now nicely warmed and put in the rice, alternating it with spoonfuls of the cheese. Drizzle with piping hot butter, stir quickly, and serve immediately, passing the pepper separately.

■ INGREDIENTS

- 450 g (14 oz) rice
- 5 tablespoons butter
- 150 g (5 oz) fontina cheese, cubed
- freshly ground white pepper (optional)

Wine: a dry red (Freisa)

Right: Risotto ai carciofi

RISOTTO CON FINOCCHI
Risotto with fennel

To make this simple and delicate risotto, it is essential to have truly tender fennel bulbs.
Be sure to discard all the tough and stringy outer leaves.

Serves 4; Preparation: 15 minutes; Cooking: 25 minutes; Level of difficulty: Simple

Cut the cleaned fennel bulbs vertically into slices about 3 mm (⅛-in) thick. § Melt 2 tablespoons of butter in a large, heavy-bottomed saucepan together with the oil. Add the onion, celery and fennel and sauté for 5-7 minutes, stirring occasionally. § Add the rice and cook for 1 minute over medium heat; then begin adding the stock, a little at a time, stirring frequently until the rice is cooked. It will take about 15-18 minutes. The risotto should be creamy but not too liquid. § Finally, add the remaining butter and the parmesan and mix well. § Season with salt and pepper and serve hot.

RISOTTO CON LE QUAGLIE
Risotto with quail

In Lombardy quail are often served with Risotto alla milanese;
a combination that works well. This one is more delicate and,
I think, more harmonious.

Serves 4; Preparation: 15 minutes; Cooking: 40 minutes; Level of difficulty: Medium

Season the quail inside and out with salt and pepper. Put the sage leaves inside. § Wrap the breasts with slices of pancetta or salt pork secured with two or three twists of white thread. § In a large, heavy-bottomed saucepan melt 1½ tablespoons of butter together with the oil. Add the quail and brown well on all sides over medium heat. This will take about 6-7 minutes. § Sprinkle the birds with the brandy and when this has evaporated, lower the heat, partially cover and cook, adding a spoonful of stock occasionally. The birds will be cooked in about 15 minutes. § Remove the quail and set aside in a warm oven or on a plate set over a pot of very hot water. § Add the rice to the juices left in the saucepan and stir well for 2 minutes. § Gradually stir in the stock. The rice will be cooked in 15-18 minutes. § At the last moment, stir in the remaining butter and the cheese. § Serve the rice with the quail arranged on top. Remove the thread but leave the salt pork or pancetta in place.

■ INGREDIENTS

- 4-5 fennel bulbs, cleaned
- 2 tablespoons butter
- 2-3 tablespoons extra-virgin olive oil
- 1 small onion, finely chopped
- 1 small stalk celery, finely chopped
- 350 g (12 oz) arborio rice
- 1 litre (1 quart) boiling beef stock (see recipe p. 24)
- salt and freshly ground white pepper
- 4 tablespoons freshly grated parmesan cheese

Wine: a dry white (Soave)

■ INGREDIENTS

- 4 quail ready to be cooked
- salt and freshly ground white pepper
- 4 leaves sage
- 4 slices salt pork or pancetta
- 3 tablespoons butter
- 2 tablespoons extra-virgin olive oil
- 3 tablespoons brandy
- 350 g (11 oz) arborio rice
- 1.2 litres (5 cups) boiling beef stock (see recipe p. 24)
- 2-3 tablespoons freshly grated parmesan cheese

Wine: a dry white (Cortese di Gavi)

Right:
Risotto con finocchi

INGREDIENTS

- 30 g (1 oz) dried porcini mushrooms
- 5 tablespoons extra-virgin olive oil
- 1 small onion, finely chopped
- 125 ml (½ cup) dry white wine
- 350 g (11 oz) arborio rice
- 1 litre (1 quart) hot vegetable stock (see recipe p. 22)
- 1 heaped tablespoon chopped parsley
- salt

Wine: a dry white
(Pinot Grigio)

RISOTTO AI FUNGHI
Mushroom risotto Venetian-style

There are many different recipes for mushroom risotto. This one comes from the city of Venice.

Serves 4; Preparation: 30 minutes; Cooking: 25-30 minutes; Level of difficulty: Medium

Soak the mushrooms for 30 minutes in 250 ml (1 cup) of tepid water. Drain, reserving the water and chop coarsely. § Strain the water in which the mushrooms were soaked and set it aside. § Heat the oil in a large, heavy-bottomed saucepan. Add the onion and sauté over low heat until it is soft and translucent. § Add the mushrooms and sauté for 2-3 minutes. § Add the rice and stir for at least 2 minutes over medium heat. Add the wine gradually and when it has all been absorbed, stir in the mushroom water. § Begin adding the hot stock a little at a time until the rice is cooked. It will take about 15-18 minutes. § Add the parsley just before the rice is cooked and mix well. § Season with salt to taste and serve hot.

VARIATION
– Add 2-3 tablespoons of freshly grated parmesan at the end, or pass separately at table.

INGREDIENTS

- 4 tablespoons butter
- 1 small onion, finely chopped
- 350 g (11 oz) arborio rice
- 100 ml (3½ fl oz) dry white wine
- 1.2 litres (5 cups) boiling chicken or beef stock (see recipes p. 24)
- pinch of nutmeg (optional)
- 4 tablespoons freshly grated parmesan cheese
- salt and freshly ground white pepper

Wine: a dry red
(Gutturnio)

Left:
Risotto ai funghi

RISOTTO BIANCO AL PARMIGIANO
Simple risotto with parmesan cheese

Serves 4; Preparation: 5 minutes; Cooking: 25 minutes; Level of difficulty: Medium

Melt 2 tablespoons of the butter in a large, heavy-bottomed saucepan. Add the onion and sauté over low heat until soft and translucent. § Add the rice, increase the heat and stir for 2 minutes. § Pour in the wine and when it has been completely absorbed, gradually stir in the stock. Stir frequently, adding the nutmeg, if liked. § When the rice is almost cooked (it will take about 15-18 minutes), add a little over half the parmesan. § Taste for salt and, finally, add the remaining butter in dabs, mixing well. § Serve with the remaining parmesan passed separately.

VARIATION
– After the wine has evaporated, add 2 tablespoons of tomato paste. This will give you *Risotto rosso alla piemontese* or "Red risotto Piedmont-style". In this case, use a little less parmesan.

Risotto ai formaggi

Cheese risotto

Many different combinations of cheeses can be used in this recipe. These four go particularly well together, but feel free to experiment with others.

Serves 4; Preparation: 15 minutes; Cooking: 35 minutes; Level of difficulty: Simple

Put the rice into 2 litres (2 quarts) of salted, boiling water and stir once or twice. Cook for 13-15 minutes. § Butter an ovenproof baking dish with 1 tablespoon of the butter. § Mix the bread crumbs with 1 tablespoon of the parmesan. § Melt 2½ tablespoons of the butter in a saucepan, add the sage or rosemary and the nutmeg and garlic, if liked. Sauté until golden brown. § When the rice is cooked, drain well and transfer to a bowl. § Stir in the cheeses and sausage. § Remove the herbs from the butter and add to the rice. Stir rapidly. § Transfer the mixture to a baking dish. Smooth the surface, sprinkle with the mixed bread crumbs and parmesan and dot with dabs of the remaining butter. § Bake in a preheated oven at 200-220°C /400-435°F for 15 minutes, or until a golden crust has formed.

INGREDIENTS

- 350 g (11 oz) arborio rice
- 4 tablespoons butter
- 1 tablespoon bread crumbs
- 5 leaves fresh or dried sage, or 1 sprig rosemary
- 1 clove garlic (optional)
- 60 g (2 oz) emmental cheese, 60 g (2 oz) smoked scamorza cheese, 60 g (2 oz) fontina cheese, finely chopped
- 60 g (2 oz) freshly grated parmesan cheese
- 150 g (5 oz) Italian pork sausage, skinned and crumbled
- pinch of nutmeg (optional)

Wine: a dry red (Cabernet)

Risotto al gorgonzola

Gorgonzola risotto

Rice and gorgonzola cheese make a tasty partnership. Choose the best soft and creamy cheese.

Serves 4; Preparation: 10 minutes; Cooking: 25 minutes; Level of difficulty: Simple

Melt the butter in a large, heavy-bottomed saucepan. § Add the onion and sauté over low heat until soft and translucent. § Add the rice and cook, stirring constantly, for 2 minutes. § Increase the heat slightly and pour in the wine. § When the wine has all been absorbed, begin adding the stock, a little at a time and stirring frequently. § The rice will take about 15-18 minutes to cook. § About 3-4 minutes before it is ready, add the gorgonzola and mix well. Season with salt and pepper. § Add the parmesan and serve.

VARIATIONS
– Replace the gorgonzola with the same quantity of well-ripened taleggio; in this case add half a finely chopped garlic clove and a dash of nutmeg to the onion before adding the rice.
– Stir in 2-3 tablespoons of fresh cream just before serving.

INGREDIENTS

- 2½ tablespoons butter
- ½ small onion, finely chopped
- 350 g (11 oz) arborio rice
- 150 ml (5 fl oz) dry white wine
- 1.2 litres (5 cups) boiling beef stock (see recipe p. 24)
- 250 g (8 oz) gorgonzola cheese, chopped
- salt and freshly ground white pepper
- 3 tablespoons freshly grated parmesan cheese

Wine: a dry red (Merlot)

Right:
Risotto al gorgonzola

Risotto con lenticchie
Creamy lentil risotto

Serves 4; Preparation: 10 minutes; Cooking: 20-25 minutes; Level of difficulty: Simple

Heat the butter and oil in a large, heavy-bottomed saucepan. Add the onion and garlic and sauté for 5 minutes over low heat. § Increase the heat slightly and pour in the rice. Cook for 2 minutes, stirring continuously. § Add the stock little by little, stirring frequently. After about 10 minutes, add the drained lentils and continue cooking. The rice will be ready in about 15-18 minutes. § Add half the cheese and season with salt and pepper. § Mix well until creamy and serve. The remaining cheese can be served separately at table.

■ INGREDIENTS

- 2½ tablespoons butter
- 3 tablespoons extra-virgin olive oil
- 1 small onion, finely chopped
- 1 small clove garlic, finely chopped
- 350 g (11 oz) arborio rice
- 1 litre (1 quart) hot beef stock (see recipe p. 24)
- 450 g (14 oz) tinned lentils
- 5 tablespoons freshly grated pecorino romano or parmesan cheese
- salt and freshly ground white or black pepper

Wine: a dry red (Rosso Conero)

Risotto con i peoci
Risotto with mussels

This recipe comes from Veneto, the region around the city of Venice. In local dialect mussels are called peoci.

Serves 4; Preparation: 20 minutes + 1 hour soaking for mussels; Cooking: 20 minutes; Level of difficulty: Medium

Soak the mussels in a large bowl of water for at least an hour to purge them of sand. Pull off their beards, scrub and rinse well in abundant cold water. § Combine the mussels and the whole clove of garlic in a large, shallow frying pan. Place over high heat and shake the frying pan and stir with a wooden spoon until all the mussels are open. This will take about 2-3 minutes. Discard any that have not opened. § Drain the mussels. Set aside a dozen of the largest, in their shells, to use as a garnish. § Take the remaining mussels out of their shells and put them in a bowl. § Strain the liquid left in the pan through a fine cloth or sieve and set it aside, discarding the garlic. § Sauté the onion and chopped garlic in the same frying pan for a few minutes. § Add the rice and cook, stirring continuously, for 2 minutes. § Increase the heat slightly and pour in the

■ INGREDIENTS

- 1 kg (2 lb) mussels
- 2 cloves garlic, 1 of which finely chopped
- 125 ml (½ cup) extra-virgin olive oil
- ½ small onion, finely chopped
- 350 g (11 oz) arborio rice
- 100 ml (3½ fl oz) dry white wine
- 750 ml (3 cups) boiling water
- salt and freshly ground pepper
- 1 heaped tablespoon of finely chopped parsley

Wine: a dry white (Tocai Isonzo)

wine. When all the wine has been absorbed, begin slowly adding the mussel liquid and then boiling water as required, stirring frequently, until the rice is cooked. This will take about 15-18 minutes. § Add the mussels and stir well. Sprinkle with the parsley and season with salt and pepper. § Transfer to a serving dish and garnish with the whole mussels. § Serve hot.

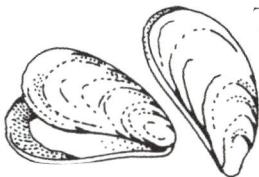

Above:
Risotto con lenticchie

VARIATION
– At the last minute add 2 tablespoons of butter and 2 heaping tablespoons of freshly grated parmesan cheese. Many consider this quite unorthodox, but the Venetians think otherwise.

RISOTTO AL LIMONE
Lemon risotto

The distinctive flavour of this risotto does not combine well with any wine.
Serve with cool, sparkling mineral water with slices of lemon.

Serves 4; Preparation: 10 minutes; Cooking: 25 minutes; Level of difficulty: Simple

Sauté the onion in the oil for a few minutes over medium-low heat in a large, heavy-bottomed saucepan until it is soft and translucent. § Increase the heat slightly and add the rice; stir for 2 minutes. § Add the wine and when it has been absorbed, gradually add the hot stock as required. § After about 10 minutes, add the lemon rind, stirring well. § The rice will take about 15-18 minutes to cook. § Season with salt and pepper to taste. Add the lemon juice and parsley, stir well and serve.

■ INGREDIENTS

- ½ small onion, finely chopped
- 4 tablespoons extra-virgin olive oil
- 350 g (11 fl oz) arborio rice
- 100 ml (3½ fl oz) dry, light white wine
- 1.2 litres (5 cups) boiling beef stock (see recipe p. 24)
- grated rind and juice of 1 large lemon
- salt and freshly ground white pepper
- juice of 1 lemon
- 1 tablespoon finely chopped parsley

RISOTTO ALLA MILANESE
Milanese-style risotto

This is a traditional Milanese dish. Debate has always raged about whether wine should be added or not (and if so, whether it should it be red or white). Try it with both, and without and decide for yourselves.

Serves 4; Preparation: 10 minutes; Cooking: 25 minutes; Level of difficulty: Medium

Melt 2 tablespoons of butter with the marrow in a large, heavy-bottomed saucepan. § Add the onion and sauté over low heat until it is soft and translucent. § Add the rice and cook over medium heat for 2-3 minutes, stirring continuously. § Pour in the wine, if used, and when it has all been absorbed, add the boiling stock, a little at a time, stirring continuously. If wine is not used, begin directly with the stock. Increase the heat slightly. § The rice will take about 15-18 minutes to cook. After 15 minutes, add half the parmesan. § Add the saffron 1 minute before the rice is ready. Taste for salt. § Add the remaining butter in dabs just before serving and mix well. The risotto should be very creamy, because of the slow and gradual release during cooking of the starch that binds the rice together. § Serve with the remaining parmesan passed separately.

■ INGREDIENTS

- 4 tablespoons butter
- 2½ tablespoons finely chopped ox-bone marrow
- 1 small onion, finely chopped
- 450 g (14 oz) arborio rice
- 125 ml (4 fl oz) white or red wine (optional)
- 1.2 litres (5 cups) boiling beef stock (see recipe p. 24)
- 6 tablespoons freshly grated parmesan cheese
- ½ teaspoon powdered saffron
- salt

Wine: a dry white (Riesling dell'Oltrepò Pavese)

VARIATION
– Add shavings of white truffle to the risotto just before serving.

Right:
Risotto al limone

■ INGREDIENTS

- 3 tablespoons butter
- 1 small onion, finely chopped
- 60 g (2 oz) diced lean pancetta
- 100 ml (3½ fl oz) dry white wine (optional)
- 350 g (11 oz) arborio rice
- 1 litre (1 quart) beef stock (see recipe p. 24)
- pinch of nutmeg
- salt and freshly ground white pepper
- 120 g (4 oz) prosciutto, cut in thick slices and cubed
- 125 ml (½ cup) light (single) cream
- 4 tablespoons freshly grated parmesan cheese

Wine: a light, dry red
(Lagrein Rosato)

■ INGREDIENTS

- 1 quantity *Risotto alla milanese* (see recipe p. 84)
- 4 tablespoons butter
- 4 tablespoons freshly grated parmesan cheese

Wine: a young, dry red
(San Colombano)

Left:
Risotto con pancetta e prosciutto

RISOTTO CON PANCETTA E PROSCIUTTO
Risotto with pancetta and prosciutto

Serves 4; Preparation: 15 minutes; Cooking: 25-30 minutes; Level of difficulty: Medium

Melt the butter in a large, heavy-bottomed saucepan, add the onion and after 1 minute the pancetta. Sauté over low heat, stirring occasionally, until the onion is soft and translucent. § Add the rice and cook for 2 minutes, stirring continuously. § Increase the heat slightly and pour in the wine. When it has all been absorbed, gradually add the hot stock as required until the rice is cooked. This will take about 15-18 minutes. § Three minutes before the rice is cooked, add a pinch of freshly grated nutmeg, pepper to taste, the ham, cream and cheese, mixing carefully to combine the ingredients well. Finally, taste for salt. § Serve hot.

VARIATIONS
— Add 2 tablespoons of butter instead of the cream.
— Emmental cheese, or scamorza or some other similar type of cheese, in flakes or shavings, can be used instead of the parmesan.

RISOTTO ALLA MILANESE 'AL SALTO'
Milanese-style risotto the day after

In Milan this was once the classic dish to order after an evening at the theatre. It is prepared with leftover Risotto alla milanese, *so make a double quantity and serve this one the day after. In the original recipe the portions are prepared individually, but since not everyone is able to deal with four frying pans at once, I have simplified things a little.*

Serves 4; Preparation: 5 minutes; Cooking: 15 minutes; Level of difficulty: Simple

Melt 1 tablespoon of the butter in each of two nonstick frying pans 30 cm (12 in) in diameter. § Divide the rice into two portions and flatten each out so as to have two round cakes about 2.5 cm (1 in) deep. § Cook them in the frying pans over high heat for about 5 minutes, so that a crisp crust forms. § Turn them with the help of a plate and slip them back into the frying pans in which you have melted the remaining butter. § When both sides are crisp and deep gold in colour, sprinkle with the parmesan and cut each one in half. § Serve immediately.

Risotto con mozzarella e panna
Risotto with mozzarella cheese and cream

Because of its delicate flavour, this recipe requires very fresh mozzarella if it is to be a success.

Serves 4; Preparation: 5 minutes; Cooking: 20-25 minutes; Level of difficulty: Simple

Melt the butter in a large, heavy-bottomed saucepan. Add the onion and sauté over low heat for a couple of minutes until the onion is soft and translucent. § Add the rice and cook for 2 minutes, stirring continuously. § Pour in the wine and when this has been absorbed, gradually add the stock, a little at a time, until two-thirds have been used. § After about 10 minutes add half the cream, stir well and then add the other half. § After 2-3 minutes add the mozzarella. § Continue cooking for about 10 minutes by which time the rice should be cooked. Stir in the remaining stock as required. § Season with salt and pepper. Serve the risotto with the grated parmesan passed separately.

■ INGREDIENTS

- 2 tablespoons butter
- 1 small onion, finely chopped
- 350 g (11 oz) arborio rice
- 125 ml (½ cup) dry white wine
- 1 litre (1 quart) beef or chicken stock (see recipe p. 24)
- 125 ml (½ cup) light cream
- 250 g (8 oz) mozzarella cheese, cubed
- salt and freshly ground white pepper
- 4 tablespoons freshly grated parmesan cheese

Wine: a dry white (Ischia Bianco)

Risotto alla piemontese
Piedmont-style risotto

Thin shavings of white truffles, sprinkled on the risotto just before serving are the perfect complement to this dish. Cooking time for the sauce is about 10 minutes, so it can be prepared when the risotto is well-advanced in its cooking and needs little attention. Ideally, the sauce and the risotto should be ready at exactly the same time.

Serves 4; Preparation: 15 minutes + 3 hours soaking; Cooking: 25 minutes; Level of difficulty: Complicated

Put the fontina in a bowl and cover it with the milk. Set aside for 3 hours. § When the fontina has been soaking for 2½ hours, prepare the risotto. § When the fontina is ready, melt the butter (which must not bubble) in a double boiler or heavy-bottomed saucepan and add the fontina and about half of the milk in which it was soaked. Stir carefully with a wooden spoon or a whisk over very low heat until the cheese melts and the mixture is runny. § Add the first egg yolk and mix thoroughly before adding the second. Repeat this procedure before adding the third, mixing rather quickly to achieve a smooth, creamy sauce. § Season with salt and pepper (if serving with truffles, add less salt and pepper than you normally would). § Transfer the risotto to a serving dish and pour the sauce over the top. § Serve immediately.

■ INGREDIENTS

- 300 g (10 oz) fontina cheese, cut in thin slices
- 250 ml (1 cup) milk
- 1 quantity *Risotto bianco al parmigiano* (see recipe p. 79)
- 3 tablespoons butter
- 3 egg yolks, at room temperature
- salt and freshly ground white pepper

Wine: a dry red (Nebbiolo)

Right:
Risotto con mozzarella e panna

Risotto all'onegliese
Risotto with tomato and mushrooms

This dish, originally from the village of Oneglia, in Liguria, has spread all along the Italian Riviera.

Serves 4; Preparation: 30 minutes; Cooking: 35 minutes; Level of difficulty: Medium

Soak the mushrooms in a bowl of warm water for about 30 minutes until they have softened; then drain and chop coarsely. § If using fresh tomatoes, plunge them for 10 seconds into a pot of boiling water and then into cold. Peel and cut them in half horizontally. Squeeze to remove at least some of the seeds and then chop finely. § If using tinned tomatoes, partially drain them and chop finely. § In a heavy-bottomed saucepan, sauté the onion in the oil until translucent. Add the mushrooms and, after another minute or so, the tomatoes. § Cook the sauce for 10 minutes, covered, then add the rice and stir well. § When part of the liquid has been absorbed, begin to add the lightly salted boiling water, pouring it in a little at a time and stirring frequently. The rice will be cooked in about 15-18 minutes. § Just before it is ready, season with salt and pepper. § Serve the rice, passing the grated cheese separately.

■ INGREDIENTS

- 20 g (⅔ oz) dried mushrooms
- 450 g (14 oz) fresh or tinned tomatoes, skinned
- 1 small onion, finely chopped
- 80 ml (3fl oz) extra-virgin olive oil
- 350 g (11 oz) arborio rice
- 1 litre (1 quart) boiling water
- salt and freshly ground black pepper
- 3 tablespoons freshly grated pecorino or parmesan cheese

Wine: a dry white (Pigato di Albenga)

Ris in cagnon
Rice with butter

A simple and pleasant dish from Lombardy, the region around Milan.

Serves 4; Preparation: 5 minutes; Cooking: 15 minutes; Level of difficulty: Simple

Cook the rice in about 2 litres (2 quarts) of salted water, stirring a couple of times until it is cooked. It will take about 13-15 minutes. § Just before the rice is ready, slowly melt the butter in a saucepan with the garlic (remove after 1 minute) and sage leaves. The butter should turn dark golden brown. § Drain the rice thoroughly and transfer to a serving dish or individual plates. § Sprinkle with the parmesan and drizzle with the hot butter, with or without the sage leaves.

■ INGREDIENTS

- 450 g (14 oz) arborio rice
- 4 tablespoons butter
- 1 clove garlic, cut in half
- 6 leaves sage (fresh or dried), whole or crumbled
- 5 tablespoons freshly grated parmesan cheese

Wine: a dry white (Lugana)

Right:
Risotto all'onegliese

Panissa
Risotto with beans

This is a hearty winter dish from the area around Vercelli, in the north. Traditionally, it is served with a generous sprinkling of pepper rather than with the usual grated cheese. If you can't get cotenna, just leave it out. The flavour will be a little different, but still very good.

Serves 4; Preparation: 30 minutes; Cooking: 1¼ hours; Level of difficulty: Medium

Put the beans in a pot with the stock and the cotenna. Cover and simmer over low heat for 50 minutes. § Take out the cotenna, dice and return to the pot. § Place the salt pork and pancetta in a heavy-bottomed saucepan over low heat. When the fat has melted a little, add the onion and sauté for 5 minutes, stirring frequently. § Pour in the rice and stir for 2 minutes. § Add the wine, half at a time. § When it has all been absorbed, begin adding, one ladle at a time, the hot beans and their broth. § Stir continuously until the rice is cooked. It will take about 15-18 minutes. § Season with salt and pepper. The risotto should be creamy but not too liquid. § Serve hot.

VARIATION
– If using dry beans, soak in cold water for 10-12 hours, then cook slowly with the cotenna for a couple of hours. Continue as above.

■ INGREDIENTS

- 250 g (8 oz) fresh cranberry or red kidney beans, shelled
- 60 g (2 oz) fresh cotenna, scraped
- 1 litre (1 quart) vegetable stock (see recipe p. 22)
- 1 small onion, finely chopped
- 60 g (2 oz) finely chopped lard
- 60 g (2 oz) finely chopped lean pancetta
- 350 g (11 oz) arborio rice
- 250 ml (1 cup) robust red wine
- salt and freshly ground white or black pepper

Wine: a dry red (Grignolino)

Risotto al vino
Risotto with wine

Choose a Barolo or a Chianti wine. The former has more body, the latter is lighter. The wine can be added about 5 tablespoons at a time, or alternately with the stock.

Serves 4; Preparation: 10 minutes; Cooking: 25 minutes; Level of difficulty: Simple

Melt 3 tablespoons of butter in a large, heavy-bottomed saucepan. Add the onion, celery and carrot and sauté over low heat for 5 minutes. § Increase the heat slightly, add the rice and cook for 2 minutes, stirring continuously. § Gradually stir in 250 ml (1 cup) of wine. § When this has been absorbed, begin adding the remaining wine and the stock, as explained above. § It will take about 15-18 minutes for the rice to cook. Season with salt and pepper. § Add the remaining butter just before serving. § The parmesan can either be added at this point or passed separately at table.

VARIATION
– For *Risotto allo champagne* use the same quantity of high quality, dry sparkling wine or champagne in place of the red wine.

■ INGREDIENTS

- 4½ tablespoons butter
- 1 small onion, finely chopped
- 1 small celery stalk, finely chopped
- 1 small carrot, scraped and finely chopped
- 350 g (11 oz) arborio rice
- 300 ml (10fl oz) Barolo or Chianti wine
- 1 litre (1 quart) boiling beef or chicken stock (see recipe p. 24)
- 4 tablespoons freshly grated parmesan cheese
- salt and freshly ground black pepper

Wine: a dry red (Gutturnio)

Right: *Panissa*

Risotto nero con le seppie
Black risotto with cuttlefish

For first-timers, the colour of this extraordinary risotto may be a little surprising. If possible, get your fishmonger to clean the cuttlefish, making sure the internal ink sacs are set aside without being broken.

Serves 4; Preparation: 25 minutes; Cooking: about 1¼ hours; Level of difficulty: Medium

To clean the cuttlefish, detach the head (the part with the tentacles) from the body by grasping the two parts with your hands and tugging sharply. The insides and two sacs will come out attached to the head. One of the sacs has the ink and the other is dark yellow. Some people also use the latter but the flavour is rather strong and it is better to discard it with the insides. Carefully separate the ink sacs from the cuttlefish and set them aside in a cup with 2-3 spoonfuls of cold water. Discard the eyes and the beaks at the base of the tentacles. Open the body at the side with kitchen scissors and extract the bone. Rinse the body and head well and cut into 3 cm (1¼ in) strips. § In a large, heavy-bottomed saucepan heat the oil and add the onion, parsley and cuttlefish. § Cover and cook for 15 minutes over low heat, stirring once or twice. § Add the tomato paste, wine and 125 ml (½ cup) hot water, and continue cooking, covered and over low heat, for 20-40 minutes, stirring occasionally. It is hard to give an exact time because this depends on the cuttlefish. Test them with a fork after 20 minutes; if they seem fairly tender, go on to the next stage (if cooked too long, cuttlefish become hard and rubbery). § In the meantime cut the ink sacs with scissors and collect the ink in a bowl, diluting with 500 ml (2 cups) of cold water. Throw the empty sacs away. § When the cuttlefish are tender, pour the black liquid into the saucepan, raise the heat slightly and bring to a boil. § Cook for 5 minutes then add the rice. § Continue cooking, stirring frequently, and adding more boiling water if the mixture becomes too dry. § The rice will take about 15-18 minutes to cook. The risotto should be very creamy. § Taste for salt and pepper and serve hot.

■ INGREDIENTS

- 2 fresh cuttlefish weighing about 750 g (1½ lb)
- 6 tablespoons extra-virgin olive oil
- 1 small onion, finely chopped
- 1 clove garlic, finely chopped
- 1 tablespoon finely chopped parsley
- 1 scant tablespoon tomato paste
- 125 ml (½ cup) dry white wine
- 350 g (11 oz) arborio rice
- salt and freshly ground white pepper

Wine: a dry white (Locorotondo)

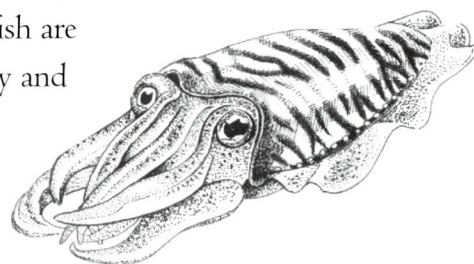

A destra:
Risotto nero con le seppie

INGREDIENTS

- 1 quantity *Milanese-style risotto* (see recipe p. 84)
- 6 chicken livers
- 2 tablespoons butter
- 125 ml (½ cup) white wine
- 1 grated lemon rind
- salt and freshly ground black pepper
- 1 tablespoon finely chopped parsley

Wine: a dry red (Nebbiolo)

RISOTTO ALLA MILANESE CON SALSA DI FEGATINI
Milanese-style risotto with chicken liver sauce

Serves 4; Preparation: 35 minutes; Cooking: 30 minutes; Level of difficulty: Medium

Prepare the Milanese-style risotto. § Wash the chicken livers under cold running water for about 30 minutes to remove all the blood. § Chop the livers coarsely and sauté in the butter for about 5 minutes over medium heat. § Add the wine and, when it evaporates, the lemon rind. Season with salt and pepper. § Place the risotto in a heated serving dish and distribute the liver sauce on top. § Sprinkle with the parsley and serve hot.

INGREDIENTS

- 3 tablespoons butter
- 1 small onion, finely chopped
- 1 celery stalk, cleaned and chopped
- 1 leek, cleaned and sliced (white part only)
- 200 g (6½ oz) fresh spinach, cleaned, cooked, squeezed dry and finely chopped
- 350 g (11 oz) arborio rice
- 1.2 litres (5 cups) boiling vegetable or beef stock (see recipes pp. 22 and 24)
- salt and freshly ground white pepper
- nutmeg (optional)
- 4 tablespoons freshly grated parmesan cheese

Wine: a dry white
(Valcalepio Bianco)

INGREDIENTS

- 300 g (10 oz) fresh cranberry or red kidney beans, shelled
- 1 small onion
- 4 leaves sage (or ½ bay leaf)
- 125 g (4 oz) green beans
- 350 g (11 oz) rice
- 5 tablespoons extra-virgin olive oil
- salt and freshly ground black pepper

Wine: a dry white
(Cortese di Gavi)

Left:
Risotto con spinaci

RISOTTO CON SPINACI
Rice with spinach

Serves 4; Preparation: 20 minutes; Cooking: 25 minutes; Level of difficulty: Medium

Melt 2 tablespoons of the butter in a large, heavy-bottomed saucepan. Add the onion, celery and leek and sauté for 3-4 minutes over low heat. § Add the spinach, stir and sauté for 2 minutes. § Add the rice and after one minute begin adding the boiling stock, a little at a time, until the rice is cooked. It will take about 15-18 minutes. § Season with salt and pepper and a pinch of nutmeg (if liked). § Add the remaining butter and the parmesan, mix carefully, and serve.

VARIATIONS
— If fresh spinach is not available, use 150 g (5 oz) of frozen spinach instead.
— Replace one-third of the parmesan with 1 tablespoon of soft, fresh ricotta cheese.
— Just before serving, add 2-3 tablespoons of cream to the risotto, in addition to (or instead of) the remaining butter.

INSALATA DI RISO E FAGIOLI
Rice and bean salad

Serves 4; Preparation: 10 minutes; Cooking: 40-50 minutes; Level of difficulty: Simple

Place the beans in a pot with the onion and sage (or bay leaf) and add enough cold water to cover them by about 5 cm (2 in). § Cover and cook over medium-low heat for about 40 minutes. Taste one to see if they are tender. § Season with salt just before removing from heat (if the salt is added earlier the skin of the beans become tough). § Clean and rinse the green beans and cut them into 2-3 pieces. § About 20-25 minutes before the cranberry or kidney beans are ready, bring a saucepan containing 2 litres (2 quarts) of salted water to a boil and add the rice and green beans. Cook over medium heat, stirring occasionally. § Drain the rice and green beans and transfer to a salad bowl. § Drain the cranberry or kidney beans. Discard the onion and sage (or bay leaf), and add to the rice, stirring rapidly. § Season with the oil and pepper. § This salad can be served hot or warm.

RISOTTO CON ZUCCA
Risotto with pumpkin

This exquisite dish of Venetian origin has almost been forgotten.
It is so delicious that it really deserves a revival.

Serves 4; Preparation: 15 minutes; Cooking: 30 minutes; Level of difficulty: Medium

Put the pumpkin in a large heavy-bottomed saucepan with the garlic, oil and half the butter. Sauté, stirring, over medium heat for 8-10 minutes. § Add the rice and cook for 2 minutes, stirring continuously. § Add the stock gradually, stirring frequently. § The pumpkin will start to disintegrate, as it should. § The rice will cook in about 15-18 minutes. It should be quite creamy when ready. § Stir in the remaining butter, the parsley, parmesan, salt and pepper, and serve immediately. § Pass extra grated parmesan separately at table.

■ INGREDIENTS

- 300 g (10 oz) Chioggia or Hubbard pumpkin, cleaned and diced
- 1 large clove garlic, finely chopped
- 3 tablespoons extra-virgin olive oil
- 3 tablespoons butter
- 350 g (11 oz) arborio rice
- 1 litre (1 quart) boiling beef stock (see recipe p. 24)
- salt and freshly ground white pepper
- 1 tablespoon finely chopped parsley
- 4 tablespoons freshly grated parmesan cheese

Wine: a light, dry red (Bardolino)

RISO IN SALSA DI ACCIUGHE
Rice in anchovy sauce

This dish combines the simple, summer flavours of the Italian Riviera with the salty taste of the open sea. Replace the salt-preserved anchovies with those kept under oil for a milder dish.

Serves 4; Preparation: 5-7 minutes; Cooking: 15 minutes; Level of difficulty: Simple

Bring 2 litres (2 quarts) of salted water to a boil. Add the rice, stir once or twice, and allow 13-15 minutes cooking time from when the water comes to a boil again. § While the rice is cooking, rinse the anchovies under cold running water and divide into fillets, removing the bones. § Rinse the capers and chop finely with the anchovies. § Heat the oil in a small frying pan, add the capers and anchovies and cook over low heat for 2-3 minutes. § Add the lemon juice just before removing from heat. § Drain the rice well and transfer to a serving dish or individual plates. Pour the sauce over the top. § Garnish with the lemon and serve hot.

■ INGREDIENTS

- 450 g (14 oz) rice
- 5 tablespoons extra-virgin olive oil
- 4 anchovies, preserved in salt
- 1 tablespoon capers
- ½ tablespoon lemon juice
- thin slices of lemon to garnish

Wine: a dry white (Cinqueterre)

Right:
Risotto con zucca

POLENTA

From its humble origins among the poorer peasants of northern Italy, polenta has gained an international reputation and a host of gourmet interpretations.

INGREDIENTS

BASIC POLENTA

(see instructions p. 16)

- 2 litres (2 quarts) boiling water
- 1 heaped tablespoon coarse sea salt
- 450 g (14 oz) coarse-grain cornmeal

INGREDIENTS

- 1 quantity BASIC POLENTA (as above)
- 1 litre (1 quart) cold milk
- 3 tablespoons fresh cream

Wine: a light, dry red (Lambrusco)

INGREDIENTS

- 1 quantity BASIC POLENTA (as above)
- 90 g (3 oz) butter
- 4 tablespoons freshly grated parmesan cheese

Wine: a dry red (Chianti Classico - Geografico)

INGREDIENTS

- 1 quantity BASIC POLENTA (as above)
- 125 g (4 oz) salt pork, 2 cloves garlic, 2 tablespoons parsley, finely chopped together

Wine: a dry red (Grignolino)

Left: *Polenta e lardo*

POLENTA CONDITA ALL'ANTICA
Polenta with traditional toppings

These simple recipes give us a taste of how polenta was served in peasant homes in times of yore. A rather soft polenta is needed, so use slightly less yellow cornmeal than in the basic recipe. Follow the quantities given here and the instructions for making polenta on p. 16.

POLENTA E LATTE
Polenta and milk

Serves 4-6; Preparation: 5 minutes; Cooking: 50-60 minutes; Level of difficulty: Simple

Pour the milk into a jug and then add the cream. § Pour the piping hot polenta into soup plates or, in the classic version, small bowls. § Serve the polenta and creamy milk separately, so that everyone can help themselves to as much as they like.

POLENTA CON BURRO E FORMAGGIO
Polenta with butter and cheese

Serves 4-6; Preparation: 5 minutes; Cooking: 50-60 minutes; Level of difficulty: Simple

Chop the butter in small pieces, dust with the parmesan and place half in individual soup plates. § Pour the polenta into the plates and sprinkle the rest of the butter and parmesan on top. § This recipe is also good with the same quantity of gorgonzola cheese instead of parmesan.

POLENTA E LARDO
Polenta and salt pork

Serves 4-6; Preparation: 5 minutes; Cooking: 50-60 minutes; Level of difficulty: Simple

Mash the chopped salt pork, garlic and parsley with the blade of a knife held flat to achieve a smooth, almost creamy, mixture. § Place half the mixture in the bottom of individual soup plates. § Pour the hot polenta into the plates and cover with the remaining mixture. § Serve.

POLENTA D'OROPA
Oropa-style polenta

*Oropa is a tiny locality in Piedmont in northern Italy. Apart from this dish,
it is also famous for its beautiful religious sanctuary.*

Serves 4; Preparation: 10 minutes; Cooking: 50 minutes; Level of difficulty: Medium

Use the first four ingredients to prepare the polenta as explained on p. 16. These quantities will make a rather soft polenta. § After the polenta has been cooking for about 30 minutes, add the toma and continue cooking for another 15 minutes, stirring energetically. § A few minutes before the polenta is cooked, slowly melt the butter in a small saucepan until it starts to bubble. § Pour the polenta into a large serving dish, dust with pepper and sprinkle with the parmesan. Drizzle the hot butter over the top and serve immediately.

VARIATION
— Toma cheese can be hard to find outside northern Piedmont. Use the same quantity of fontina or fontal in its place.

■ INGREDIENTS

- 1 litre (1 quart) boiling water
- 1 litre (1 quart) hot milk
- 1 tablespoon coarse sea salt
- 300 g (10 oz) coarse-grain cornmeal
- 450 g (14 oz) toma grassa cheese, cut in slivers
- 5 tablespoons freshly grated parmesan cheese
- 6 tablespoons butter
- freshly ground black pepper

*Wine: a dry red
(Gamay della Valle d'Aosta)*

POLENTA DI PATATE
Potato polenta

This delicious polenta comes from Trento in the northeast. It should be served with pickles, particularly sweet-sour gherkins. For a complete meal, serve with grilled or baked pork ribs.

Serves 4; Preparation: 30 minutes; Cooking: 30-35 minutes; Level of difficulty: Medium

Mash the potatoes and transfer to the pot where the polenta is to be cooked. § Add the cornmeal and buckwheat flour, mix well, and continue to mix while adding the water. § Cook over medium-high heat, stirring frequently and energetically. § Melt the butter and oil over medium heat in a small saucepan. Add the onion and sauté until golden. § Add the butter and oil to the polenta which will have been cooking for about 10 minutes by this time. Stir continuously. § After 20 more minutes, add a little salt, a generous pinch or two of pepper, and the cheese and continue stirring for 10 more minutes. § Serve immediately. If there is any left over, cut in slices when cold and grill or fry.

VARIATIONS
— Fine grain yellow cornmeal can also be used.
— If you don't have buckwheat flour use a double quantity of cornmeal.

■ INGREDIENTS

- 1 kg (2 lb) potatoes, boiled and peeled, still hot
- 60 g (2 oz) coarse-grain cornmeal
- 60 g (2 oz) buckwheat flour
- 250 ml (1 cup) boiling water
- 2 tablespoons butter
- 3 tablespoons extra-virgin olive oil
- 1 large onion, thinly sliced
- salt and freshly ground black pepper
- 125 g (4 oz) fresh Asiago cheese, cut in slivers

*Wine: a hearty, dry red
(Breganze Rosso)*

Right:
Polenta d'Oropa

Polenta con la luganega
Polenta with luganega sausage

Luganega is a type of long fresh pork sausage found throughout northern Italy. If you can't find it, use another type of fresh Italian pork sausage and modify method accordingly.

Serves 4; Preparation: 5 minutes; Cooking: 50 minutes; Level of difficulty: Medium

Prepare the polenta. § About 20 minutes before the polenta is cooked, pierce holes about 2.5 cm (1 in) apart in the casing of the luganega with a toothpick, so that the fat will drain out during cooking and the heat will penetrate to the inside. Don't use a fork as the holes will be too close together and the casing will probably break. § Roll the luganega up in a flat spiral, piercing it horizontally with two long thin wooden or metal skewers, placed crosswise, so it will keep its shape. § Melt the butter in a frying pan. Add the oil and rosemary and then carefully add the sausage. Brown for 3-4 minutes over medium heat, then turn so it will brown on the other side. § Increase the heat and pour the wine into the pan; as soon as it is hot, lower the heat and cover the pan. § Sauté for about 10 minutes, turning the luganega again after the first 5 minutes. § When it is cooked, remove the skewers and cut the sausage into pieces about 5 cm (2 in) long. § Transfer the polenta to a large serving dish and arrange the sausage pieces on top. § Discard the rosemary from the pan and drizzle the juices over the polenta and sausage. § Serve hot.

■ INGREDIENTS

- 1 quantity basic polenta (see recipe p. 16)
- 500 g (1 lb) luganega (or very fresh Italian pork sausage)
- 2 tablespoons butter
- 1 tablespoon extra-virgin olive oil
- 1 small branch rosemary
- 125 ml (½ cup) dry white or red wine

Wine: a dry red (Raboso del Piave)

Polenta al taleggio
Polenta with taleggio cheese

Taleggio cheese comes from Lombardy. It should be creamy, fragrant and well ripened. If you can't get taleggio, use the same quantity of fontina cheese in its place.

Serves 4; Preparation: 10 minutes; Cooking: 1 hour; Level of difficulty: Simple

Use the first four ingredients to prepare the polenta as explained on p. 16. These quantities will make a rather soft polenta which will cook in about 45 minutes. § Lightly butter an ovenproof baking dish about 25 cm (10 in) in diameter and about 7.5 cm (3 in) deep. § When the polenta is ready, pour one-third into the dish, sprinkle with one-third of the parmesan, one-third of the taleggio and one-third of the remaining butter, in dabs. Repeat this procedure twice. § Bake in a preheated oven at 200°C/400°F for about 15 minutes, or until the surface turns golden brown. § Serve hot.

■ INGREDIENTS

- 1.2 litres (5 cups) boiling water
- 750 ml (3 cups) milk
- 1 tablespoon coarse sea salt
- 350 g (11 oz) coarse-grain cornmeal
- 3 tablespoons butter
- 60 g (2 oz) parmesan cheese, flaked
- 300 g (10 oz) ripe taleggio cheese, sliced

Wine: a hearty, dry red (Valcalepio Rosso)

Right:
Polenta con la luganega

■ INGREDIENTS

- 2 litres (2 quarts) boiling water
- 1 tablespoon coarse sea salt
- 300 g (10 oz) coarse-grain cornmeal
- 150 g (5 oz) lean pancetta, diced
- 90 g (3 oz) freshly grated pecorino cheese
- 3 tablespoons butter
- 500 g (1 lb) tomatoes
- ½ small onion, finely chopped
- 3 tablespoons extra-virgin olive oil
- ½ clove garlic, finely chopped (optional)
- 10 fresh basil leaves, torn

Wine: a dry red
(Montescudaio Rosso)

■ INGREDIENTS

- 2 litres (2 quarts) hot water
- 1 tablespoon coarse sea salt
- 350 g (11 oz) coarse-grain cornmeal
- 1 tablespoon extra-virgin olive oil
- 300 g (10 oz) fresh Italian pork sausage, skinned and crumbled
- 90 g (3 oz) finely chopped salt pork
- ½ tablespoon finely chopped rosemary leaves
- 1 clove garlic, finely chopped
- 5 tablespoons freshly grated parmesan cheese

Wine: a dry red
(Merlot Colli Bolognesi)

Left: *Polenta alla Tosco-Emiliana*

POLENTA ALLA MAREMMANA
Maremma-style polenta

Serves 4; Preparation: 15 minutes; Cooking: 50 minutes; Level of difficulty: Simple

Use the first three ingredients to prepare the polenta as explained on p. 16. These quantities will make a very soft polenta. § Meanwhile prepare the sauce. Plunge the tomatoes into boiling water for 10 seconds, then into cold. Peel and chop coarsely. If using tinned tomatoes, do not drain but chop them slightly. § In a saucepan, over low heat, sauté the onion in the oil until it is translucent. Add the garlic, tomatoes and basil. § Turn up the heat a little and simmer the sauce for 15-20 minutes. § When the polenta is half cooked, add the pancetta, cheese and pieces of butter; stir frequently. § When the polenta is ready, transfer to individual plates and spoon the tomato sauce over the top. § Serve hot.

POLENTA ALLA TOSCO-EMILIANA
Tuscan-Emilian-style polenta

A hearty, winter dish. Followed by a salad and fruit, it is a complete meal.

Serves 4; Preparation: 15 minutes; Cooking: 1 hour, 10 minutes; Level of difficulty: Medium

Use the first three ingredients to prepare the polenta as explained on p. 16. These quantities will make a very soft polenta which will cook in about 45 minutes. § Oil an ovenproof baking dish large enough to contain the polenta in a 2.5 cm (1-in) layer. § Using a fork, carefully mix the sausage, salt pork, rosemary and garlic together in a bowl. § When the polenta is cooked, pour it into the baking dish and smooth it out with a spatula. § Spread with the sausage mixture, gently pushing it into the polenta with your fingertips. § Bake in preheated oven at 200-225°C/400-425°F, for 15 minutes. § Dust with the parmesan just before serving.

VARIATION
– If salt pork is not liked, omit and add extra sausage.

POLENTA PASTICCIATA ALLA MILANESE
Baked polenta, Milanese-style

Serves 4; Preparation: 1 hour; Cooking: 25-30 minutes; Level of difficulty: Medium

For the mushroom sauce: soak the mushrooms in 250 ml (1 cup) of tepid water for 30 minutes. Drain (reserving the liquid), squeeze out excess moisture and chop coarsely. § Strain the water in which the mushrooms were soaked and set aside. § In a small frying pan melt the butter and sauté the onion for a few minutes over low heat; add the sausage, the mushrooms with 3-4 spoonfuls of their water and the tomatoes. If not using the tomatoes, add all the mushroom water (about 180 ml/6fl oz). § Cover and cook over medium heat for 30 minutes, stirring occasionally. Season with salt and pepper. (This sauce can be prepared ahead of time). § Prepare the béchamel sauce. § Butter an ovenproof baking dish about 20 cm (8 in) in diameter and 7.5 cm (3 in) deep. Cover the bottom with 6 mm (¼-in) thick slices of polenta. § Pour on one-third of the mushroom sauce, dust with one-third of the parmesan, arrange one-third of the gruyère on top and cover with one-third of the béchamel sauce. Repeat this procedure twice. § Bake in a preheated oven at 200-230°C/400-450°F for 25-30 minutes, or until the top is golden. § Serve hot.

POLENTA PASTICCIATA AL FORMAGGIO
Baked polenta with cheese

*Always make a generous quantity of polenta,
there are so many delicious ways of using up any that is leftover.*

Serves 4; Preparation: 10 minutes; Cooking: 25-30 minutes; Level of difficulty: Simple

Cut the polenta into 6 mm (¼-in) thick slices, about 5 cm (2 in) long. § Butter an ovenproof baking dish deep enough for three layers of polenta. § Cover the bottom with slices of polenta, sprinkle with one-third of the parmesan, one-third of the gruyère and dot with one-third of the butter. § Repeat this procedure twice. § Bake in a preheated oven at 200-220°C/400-425°F for 25-30 minutes, or until a golden crust has formed.

■ INGREDIENTS

SAUCE:
- 30 g (1 oz) dried porcini mushrooms
- 2 tablespoons butter
- 1 small onion, finely chopped
- 125 g (4 oz) Italian pork sausage, skinned and crumbled
- 200 g (6½ oz) peeled and chopped tinned tomatoes (optional)
- salt and freshly ground black pepper
- 1 quantity béchamel sauce (see recipe p. 24)
- 1 tablespoon butter
- 500 g (1 lb) cold polenta
- 90 g (3 oz) freshly grated parmesan cheese
- 100 g (3½ oz) gruyère cheese (or similar cheese), thinly sliced

*Wine: a dry red
(Bonarda Oltrepò Pavese)*

■ INGREDIENTS

- 500 g (1 lb) cold polenta
- 90 g (3 oz) butter
- 6 tablespoons freshly grated parmesan cheese
- 125 g (4 oz) gruyère cheese cut in slivers

*Wine: a dry red
(Donnaz)*

Right:
Polenta pasticciata alla milanese

POLENTA PASTICCIATA CON IL POMODORO
Baked polenta with tomato sauce

INGREDIENTS

- 1 quantity basic tomato sauce (see recipe p. 22)
- 1 tablespoon extra-virgin olive oil
- 500 g (1 lb) cold polenta
- 300 g (10 oz) mild provolone cheese, diced
- freshly ground black pepper (optional)

Wine: a light, dry red (San Colombano)

Serves 4; Preparation: 20 minutes; Cooking: 25-30 minutes; Level of difficulty: Simple

Prepare the tomato sauce. § Oil an ovenproof baking dish about 20 cm (8 in) in diameter and about 7.5 cm (3 in) deep. § Cover the bottom with 6 mm (¼-in) thick, short slices of the cold polenta, and scatter one-third of the diced provolone evenly on top. § Dust with pepper and drizzle with one-third of the tomato sauce. § Repeat this procedure twice, finishing up with a layer of sauce. § Bake in a preheated oven at 200-220°C/400-425°F for 25-30 minutes. § Serve piping hot straight from the oven.

POLENTA ALLA PIZZAIOLA
Polenta with pizza sauce

INGREDIENTS

- 1.8 litres (1¾ quarts) boiling water
- 1 tablespoon coarse sea salt
- 350 g (11 oz) coarse-grain cornmeal
- 4 tablespoons extra-virgin olive oil
- 250 g (8 oz) scamorza cheese, diced
- 8 anchovy fillets, preserved in oil, crumbled

Children particularly love this dish. It is also convenient because it can be prepared a few hours ahead, kept at room temperature, and then popped into the oven 20 minutes before serving.

Serves 4; Preparation: 10 minutes; Cooking: 1¼ hours; Level of difficulty: Medium

Use the first three ingredients to prepare the polenta as explained on p. 16. Cook for 50 minutes; it should be fairly solid but not too hard. § In the meantime prepare the sauce: cook the tomatoes in a small saucepan for 5 minutes over medium heat. § Add the garlic, oregano and a little salt. Cover and cook over low heat for 15 minutes, stirring occasionally. § When the sauce is cooked, add the oil. The sauce can also

Right:
Polenta pasticciata con il pomodoro

SAUCE:
- 450 g (14 oz) fresh or tinned tomatoes, partially drained and coarsely chopped
- 1 small clove garlic, finely chopped
- 1 teaspoon oregano
- salt
- 2 tablespoons extra-virgin olive oil

Wine: a dry white (Greco di Tufo)

also be prepared ahead of time. § Oil an ovenproof baking dish large enough for a layer of polenta about 2.5 cm (1 in) thick with 2 tablespoons of the oil. § When the polenta is ready, transfer it to the dish and level with a spatula. § Cover the surface with the sauce. Distribute the diced scamorza evenly on top, add the anchovy and drizzle with the remaining oil. § Cook in a preheated oven at 200°C/400°F for about 15 minutes. § If the dish was prepared ahead of time and the polenta is no longer hot, preheat the oven to 180°C/350°F and cook at that temperature for the first 10-15 minutes, then increase to 200°C/400°F for the last 5-10 minutes, otherwise a tough, unpleasant crust might form on the scamorza.

POLENTA PASTICCIATA IN SALSA DI FORMAGGIO
Baked polenta in cheese sauce

Serves 4; Preparation: 20 minutes; Cooking: 30 minutes; Level of difficulty: Simple

Melt the butter in a saucepan. When it stops foaming, add the flour and cook over low heat for a couple of minutes, stirring well. § Begin to add the milk, a little at a time, stirring continuously. The sauce should be a smooth and fluid béchamel. Season with a grating of nutmeg and pepper. § Turn up the heat and add the cheeses, a handful at a time. Keep stirring so that they will melt and the sauce will stay smooth. § Butter an ovenproof baking dish large enough to contain the polenta and sauce in a layer about 5 cm (2 in) thick. § Cut the polenta into 2 cm (¾-in) cubes. § Cover the bottom with half the polenta cubes and pour half the sauce over the top. Arrange the remaining polenta on top and cover with the remaining sauce. § Bake in a preheated oven at 200-220°C/400-425°F for 25-30 minutes, or until the top has a golden crust.

POLENTA CON I FUNGHI
Polenta with mushroom sauce

For a really tasty sauce, use highly prized wild mushrooms, such as porcini, shiitake or chanterelle. If using cultivated varieties, combine with 30 g (1 oz) of dried porcini mushrooms. Soak the dried porcini in a bowl of warm water for 30 minutes, chop coarsely and mix with the fresh mushrooms. The distinctive musky flavour of the dried porcini will add just the right amount of zest to the sauce.

Serves 4; Preparation: 20 minutes; Cooking: 50 minutes; Level of difficulty: Medium

Prepare the polenta. § To prepare the sauce: trim the stems of the mushrooms, rinse under cold running water and pat dry with kitchen towels. Slice thinly. § Heat the oil in a frying pan over medium heat, add the garlic and sauté for 2-3 minutes, stirring often so that they don't burn. Discard. § Add the parsley (or calamint) and mushrooms and cook over high heat for 2-3 minutes. § Add the tomatoes and continue cooking over medium heat for 15-20 minutes, stirring frequently. § Transfer the polenta to a serving dish and pour the mushroom sauce over the top. § Serve hot.

Right: Polenta con i funghi

Polenta Taragna
Taragna polenta

This is a typical dish of the Valtellina, in Lombardy in the north. Truly hearty, it is made with buckwheat flour, once considered to be quite lowly, but now rising in popularity.

Serves 4; Preparation: 5 minutes; Cooking: 50 minutes; Level of difficulty: Medium

Bring the water and salt to a boil. § Sift in the flour, stirring with a wire whisk and add half the butter. § Cook, stirring frequently, as for a regular polenta (see p. 16), for 40 minutes. The buckwheat polenta will be rather soft. § Add the cheese and continue stirring over fairly low heat. § After a couple of minutes add the remaining butter. § After another 5-8 minutes the polenta will be ready. Not all the cheese will have melted and combined with the polenta. § Serve immediately.

VARIATION
– Replace 100 g (3½ oz) of the buckwheat flour with the same quantity of cornmeal.

■ INGREDIENTS

- 1.5 litres (1½ quarts) water
- 1 scant tablespoon coarse salt
- 300 g (10 oz) buckwheat flour
- 200 g (7 oz) butter
- 200 g (7 oz) fontina, asiago or fontal cheese (or a mixture of the three), cut in slivers

Wine: a hearty red (Valcalepio Rosso)

Polenta fritta
Fried polenta

Leftover polenta, cut into slices about 2 cm (¾-in) thick and fried, is delicious with many meat or game dishes. It also makes an ideal snack or appetiser by itself or with various toppings. Try it with any of the meat or tomato sauces on pp. 22-26 or with the mushroom sauce given on p. 114.

Serves 4; Preparation: 2 minutes; Cooking: 8 minutes; Level of difficulty: Simple

Heat enough lard or oil and butter in a frying pan to cover the bottom by 6 mm (¼-in). § Add the rosemary, sage and garlic. When the fat is hot, but not smoking, add the slices of polenta. § As soon as they are crisp and golden underneath, turn them over with a spatula and fry on the other side. It will take about 6-8 minutes. § Lift to let excess fat drip off and transfer to paper towels to absorb the rest. § Serve with a sprinkling of salt and pepper.

VARIATION
– Fry the slices as above in oil only and omit the rosemary, sage, garlic, salt and pepper. When cooked, sprinkle with sugar and a little cinnamon and serve as a sweet or snack. This used to be a classic treat for children.

■ INGREDIENTS

- lard, or olive oil and butter, for frying
- 1 sprig rosemary
- 4 sage leaves
- 1 clove garlic
- 4-8, or more, slices of cold polenta
- salt and freshly ground black pepper

Wine: a dry red (Chianti Classico)

Right:
Polenta fritta

CROSTONI DI POLENTA AL FORMAGGIO
Fried polenta with cheese topping

Use your imagination in making these slices of fried polenta, depending on what kinds of cheese are available and how much you want to use. Some good cheeses are: taleggio, gorgonzola, fontina, asiago, provola and scamorza (smoked or plain).

Serves 4; Preparation: 10 minutes; Cooking: 8 minutes; Level of difficulty: Simple

To prepare the cheese(s), remove the crust and chop into pieces if soft, or in thin slices if harder. § Pour the oil into a frying pan and when it is hot, but not smoking, add the slices of polenta together with the sage or rosemary. § Fry over high heat for 3 minutes or so. Turn the slices over with a spatula and cover with the cheese, leaving a small border around the edges. § Cover the frying pan and cook for another 3 minutes so that the slices of polenta get crisp on the underside and the cheese melts. § Serve immediately, with a sprinkling of pepper if liked.

> VARIATION
> – Slices of Crescenza, or other very soft, fresh cheese with no crust can also be used. Brush with extra-virgin olive oil and add a generous sprinkling of pepper. In this case put the cheese on the polenta only for about 1 minute before the polenta is cooked.

■ INGREDIENTS

- 8 or more slices of cold polenta, 2 cm (¾-in) thick and about 10 cm (4 in) long
- 6 tablespoons extra-virgin olive oil
- 4 sage leaves or 1 sprig rosemary
- cheese (see introduction to recipe for types of cheese)
- freshly ground white or black pepper (optional)

Wine: a dry red (Franciacorta Rosso)

POLENTA E FAGIOLI
Polenta and beans

This recipe comes from Veneto, the region around Venice, and ideally the marbled pink and white Lamon beans (a type of red kidney bean) should be used, but they are not easy to find. Use cranberry or red kidney beans in their place.

Serves 4; Preparation: 5 minutes; Cooking: 1¼ hours; Level of difficulty: Medium

Put the beans in a pot that can hold about 5 litres (5 quarts). Add the onion, pancetta and bay leaf with enough cold water to cover the beans by at least 5 cm (2 in). § Cover and cook over low heat for about 30 minutes. § Sift the

■ INGREDIENTS

- 200 g (7 oz) fresh cranberry or red kidney beans, shelled
- ½ small onion, finely chopped
- 30 g (1 oz) finely chopped pancetta
- 1 bay leaf

Right:
Crostoni di polenta al formaggio

- 300 g (10 oz) fine-grain cornmeal
- salt
- 4 tablespoons butter
- 4 heaped tablespoons freshly grated parmesan cheese

Wine: a dry, fragrant red (Gutturnio)

cornmeal into the pot very slowly, stirring with a whisk so no lumps will form. When all the cornmeal has been added, continue stirring with a long wooden spoon. § It will take about 40 minutes for the polenta to cook. It should be very soft; if it is too hard, add a little more boiling water. § Season with salt when almost cooked. § Shortly before the polenta is cooked, melt the butter in a small saucepan to a golden colour. § Serve the polenta in individual plates, sprinkle with parmesan and drizzle with the hot butter.

VARIATION
— The following may be added before serving: sauté 1 small finely chopped onion in 6 tablespoons of extra-virgin olive oil. After a few minutes, add 4 anchovy fillets preserved in oil and stir occasionally until the onion is soft and golden.

Index